365 Ultimate Fruit Salad Recipes

(365 Ultimate Fruit Salad Recipes - Volume 1)

Lena Jones

Content

CHAPTER 3: AWESOME FRUIT SALAD RECIPES 75

Chapter 1: Orange Salad Recipes

***

1. ARUGULA SALAD WITH ORANGES POMEGRANATE SEEDS AND GOAT CHEESE Recipe

Serving: 10 | Prep: | Cook: |Ready in:

Ingredients

- 5 oranges
- 14 ounces arugula (about 16 cups)
- 3/4 cup pomegranate seeds or dried cranberries
- 1 5.5-ounce package soft fresh goat cheese, crumbled (about 1 cup)
- 1/3 cup finely chopped red onion
- Dressing:
- 3/4 cup extra-virgin olive oil
- 1/4 cup fresh lemon juice
- 2 tablespoons thawed frozen orange juice concentrate
- 3/4 teaspoon coarse salt
- 1/2 teaspoon ground black pepper

Direction

- Cut off peel and white pith from oranges
- Cut oranges into 1/4- to 1/2-inch-thick rounds; cut each round into quarters
- Transfer orange pieces to large bowl
- Add remaining ingredients and toss to combine
- Toss salad with enough dressing to coat and serve
- Dressing:

- Whisk last 5 ingredients in bowl to blend. (Can be made 1 day ahead. Chill. Bring to room temperature and rewhisk before using.)

2. Almond Orange Tossed Salad Recipe

Serving: 8 | Prep: | Cook: 15mins |Ready in:

Ingredients

- 2 tablespoons sugar
- 1/2 cup sliced almonds
- 4 cups torn iceberg lettuce
- 4 cups torn romaine
- 1 (11 ounce) can mandarin oranges, drained
- 1 large ripe avocado, peeled and cubed
- 1/2 cup diced celery
- 2 green onions, sliced
- DRESSING:
- 1/4 cup vegetable oil
- 2 tablespoons sugar
- 2 tablespoons cider vinegar
- 2 teaspoons minced fresh parsley
- 1/4 teaspoon salt
- 1/4 teaspoon pepper

Direction

- 1. In a small skillet over medium-low heat, cook sugar, without stirring for 12-14 minutes or until melted. Add almonds; stir quickly to coat. Remove from the heat; pour onto waxed paper to cool.
- 2. In a large serving bowl, combine the ice berg lettuce, romaine, oranges, avocado, celery, onions and almonds. In a jar with a tight-fitting lid, combine the dressing ingredients; shake well. Drizzle over salad; toss gently to coat.

3. Apple Orange Romaine Salad Recipe

Serving: 12 | Prep: | Cook: | Ready in:

Ingredients

- DRESSING
- 1 cup vegetable oil
- 1/3 cup cider vinegar
- 1/4 cup sugar
- 1 teaspoon celery salt
- 1/4 teaspoon black pepper
- SALAD MIX
- 1 pound spinach, stems removed
- 1 head romaine lettuce
- 2 each granny smith apples, Cored and diced
- 15 ounces mandarin orange, 1 can drained
- 1/2 cup cashew pieces
- 1/4 cup cheese, optional (I use goat cheese but make it your choice)

Direction

- Dry roast the cashews in a hot skillet for about 3 minutes. Set aside to cool. Buy cashew halves & pieces since you are going to chop them up anyway.
- In a small bowl whisk together the oil, vinegar, sugar, celery salt and pepper. Set aside.
- Chop the cashews into small pieces, not dust. Pull the leaves off of the head of romaine and tear into pieces along with the spinach leaves.
- In a large bowl combine spinach, romaine, apples, oranges and cashews.
- Serve with dressing and top with your favorite shredded cheese.

4. Apple Orange Salad Recipe

Serving: 6 | Prep: | Cook: | Ready in:

Ingredients

- 11 ounce can mandarin oranges

- 2 large apples
- 1/4 cup walnuts
- 1/2 cup orange yogurt
- 2 Tbsp orange marmalade

Direction

- Ahead of time, put the can of oranges in the refrigerator to chill.
- When you are ready to prepare, drain the oranges.
- Core the apples and cut into bite-size pieces. Don't peel unless you don't want peel in your salad.
- Break up walnuts into small pieces.
- Stir together oranges, apples and walnuts.
- Mix the yogurt and marmalade together well then toss with the fruit.

5. Artichoke And Orange Salad Recipe

Serving: 6 | Prep: | Cook: | Ready in:

Ingredients

- 24 baby artichokes
- 4 large oranges
- 3 tablespoons extra-virgin olive oil
- 2 tablespoons balsamic vinegar
- 1 small red onion, thinly sliced
- 3/4 cup kalamata olives or other brine-cured black olives

Direction

- Clean artichokes.
- Cook in large pot of boiling salted water 4 minutes.
- Drain and cool.
- Cut into thin slices.
- Grate enough orange peel to measure 1 teaspoon. Transfer peel to large bowl.
- Squeeze 1/3 cup juice from 1 orange into the bowl.

- Using a small sharp knife, cut off peel and white pith from remaining oranges.
- Cut oranges crosswise into 1/4-inch-thick slices; set aside.
- Mix oil and vinegar into orange juice mixture in bowl.
- Season with salt and pepper to your taste.
- Mix in artichokes and onion.
- Let stand 10 minutes.
- Using slotted spoon, arrange artichokes and onions on platter. Garnish with orange slices and olives.
- Drizzle vinaigrette from bowl over salad.

6. Arugula Orange Salad With Toasted Walnut Dressing Recipe

Serving: 4 | Prep: | Cook: 12mins | Ready in:

Ingredients

- 1 large bag, or 2 small, arugula (also known as rocket or rucola) greens
- 1 large seedless orange
- 1/2 cup toasted walnuts, cooled and chopped coarsely
- 4-6 oz. fresh parmesan cheese (NOT grated)
- Dressing:
- 1/2 cup walnut oil
- Scant 1/4 cup walnut vinegar (or use apple)
- 2 TBS water
- orange juice
- 1/2 small red onion, finely chopped
- 1 TBS coarse-grain mustard
- 2 TBS maple syrup
- 1 TBS sugar
- 1 tsp. salt
- Fresh-ground black pepper to taste

Direction

- If not ready-washed, wash and dry the arugula.

- Peel the orange and, catching and reserving all the juices, section and cut into small bits.
- Slice the Parmesan very thinly into flakes. Do not grate.
- Toss these ingredients along with the walnuts in a large, deep bowl.
- Combine all dressing ingredients, including reserved orange juice, in a tightly sealed jar and shake until emulsified.
- Just before serving, pour over the dressing and toss again.

7. Asian Salad With Tangy Orange Dressing Recipe

Serving: 6 | Prep: | Cook: 25mins | Ready in:

Ingredients

- 1 box of Tyson chicken tenders
- 2 cups of baby spinach (washed, dried, and drained)
- 2 cups of romaine lettuce (washed, dried, drained and chopped)
- 2 cups of arugula (washed, dried, drained, and chopped)
- 2 cups of shred carrots
- 1 red pepper seeded and thinly sliced
- 1 english cucumber (peeled and sliced)
- 1 cup of button mushroom slices (canned works well also)
- 1 cup of snow pea pods
- 1 can of water chesnut slices (drained)
- 1/2 cup of soy sauce
- 1/2 cup of EVOO
- 1/2 cup of orange marmalade
- 2 tsp of white wine vinegar
- 1 tsp of garlic powder
- 1/2 cup of slivered almonds
- 1/2 cup of crispy chow mein noodles
- salt and pepper to taste

Direction

- Prepare chicken tenders according to package directions. When they are done, slice into bite sized pieces.
- In a medium bowl combine soy sauce, EVOO, marmalade, vinegar and garlic powder and salt and pepper. Wisk together well.
- In a large salad bowl combine greens and other veggies.
- Add in chicken tenders and dressing. Toss well.
- Sprinkle with almonds and chow mein noodles. Serve.

8. Asian Spinach Salad With Orange And Avocado Recipe

Serving: 4 | Prep: | Cook: | Ready in:

Ingredients

- 2 tablespoons finely chopped shallots
- 2 tablespoons seasoned rice vinegar
- 1 tablespoon vegetable oil
- 2 teaspoons minced peeled fresh ginger
- 1/4 teaspoon (generous) Asian sesame oil
- 1 navel orange
- 1 6-ounce bag baby spinach leaves
- 1 Pinkerton or Fuerte avocado, halved, pitted, peeled, cut into 1/2-inch wedges

Direction

- Whisk first 5 ingredients in large bowl.
- Season to taste with salt and pepper.
- Set dressing aside.
- Cut off peel and white pith from orange.
- Cut orange into 1/3-inch rounds; cut rounds crosswise in half.
- Add spinach to dressing; toss to coat.
- Add avocado and orange; toss gently.

9. Asian Spinach Salad With Orange And Avocado Recipe

Serving: 4 | Prep: | Cook: | Ready in:

Ingredients

- 2 tablespoons finely chopped shallots
- 2 tablespoons seasoned rice vinegar
- 1 tablespoon vegetable oil
- 2 teaspoons minced peeled fresh ginger
- 1/4 teaspoon (generous) Asian sesame oil
- 1 navel orange
- 1 6-ounce bag baby spinach leaves
- 1 Pinkerton or Fuerte avocado, halved, pitted, peeled, cut into 1/2-inch wedges

Direction

- Whisk first 5 ingredients in large bowl.
- Season to taste with salt and pepper.
- Set dressing aside.
- Cut off peel and white pith from orange.
- Cut orange into 1/3-inch rounds; cut rounds crosswise in half.
- Add spinach to dressing; toss to coat.
- Add avocado and orange; toss gently.

10. Asparagus Boston Lettuce And Orange Salad Recipe

Serving: 6 | Prep: | Cook: 5mins | Ready in:

Ingredients

- 2 heads boston lettuce washed and torn
- 1 large red onion sliced and separated into rings
- 2 large seedless oranges peeled and cut crosswise into slices
- 1 pound fresh asparagus spears blanched
- 1/2 cup creamy poppy seed dressing

Direction

- Cover large serving platter with lettuce then top with onions and oranges.
- Add asparagus to a large pot of boiling water then cook 3 minutes and drain.
- Immediately plunge asparagus into a bowl of ice water to stop the cooking.
- When completely cool and pat dry then place asparagus on top of lettuce.
- Drizzle with dressing and serve immediately.

11. Avocado And Orange Salad Recipe

Serving: 6 | Prep: | Cook: |Ready in:

Ingredients

- fresh spinach leaves washed and dried
- 5 tiny red potatoes cooked and cooled
- 1 bunch radishes trimmed and thinly sliced
- 2 tablespoons balsamic vinegar
- 6 tablespoons extra virgin olive oil
- 1-1/2 teaspoons granulated sugar
- 1-1/2 teaspoons fresh orange zest
- 2 oranges peeled and sliced
- 1 avocado peeled and sliced

Direction

- Combine spinach, potatoes and radishes in large bowl.
- Whisk vinegar and oil in small glass measuring cup adding sugar and orange zest.
- Season with salt and pepper and pour over the salad then gently toss.
- Mound salad on large platter and top with orange and avocado slices.

12. Beet And Orange Salad Recipe

Serving: 4 | Prep: | Cook: 60mins |Ready in:

Ingredients

- 1 pound beets
- 2-3 navel (seedless) oranges
- 1 Tbsp chives, chopped (optional)
- olive oil
- balsamic vinegar
- salt
- pepper

Direction

- Scrub beets clean and trim off any greens. Rub with olive oil, if desired, wrap in aluminum foil, and roast in a 400°F oven until tender, approximately 1 hour. (Larger beets will take longer.)
- Cool beets until they can be handled.
- In the meantime, cut the peel from the oranges and section. Squeeze out juices from leftover membranes and reserve.
- Slip beets from their skins and into cubes of approximately 1/2 inch.
- Make approximately 1/4 cup vinaigrette with the orange juice, vinegar, olive oil, salt, and pepper. (Suggested: half juice/vinegar, half oil.)
- Toss together beets, orange slices, and vinaigrette. Just before serving, garnish with chives.

13. Black Bean Corn And Mandarin Salad Recipe

Serving: 6 | Prep: | Cook: |Ready in:

Ingredients

- 2 cans black beans (about 3-3.5 cups, rinsed and drained)
- 2 cans sweet yellow corn (about 3.5 cups, drained)
- 2 small cans mandarin oranges (1.5-2 cups, drained)
- 1 clove elephant garlic

- 1 jalapeno, seeded and finely chopped
- ~2 tsp cilantro, finely chopped
- ~1 tsp salt

Direction

- Mix all ingredients together.
- Eat immediately, or chill for later.
- Some notes: A batch will stay good in the refrigerator for at least one week. The elephant garlic is a little less intense than regular garlic, so using lots of it is no problem, at least for me. Trader Joe's has packs of frozen cilantro, which I find very useful. (I use 2-3 of the little cubes for one batch of this salad) You could leave the seeds in or use more jalapeno for more spice, but I'm happy with it as is.

14. Black Bean Salad With Oranges Recipe

Serving: 4 | Prep: | Cook: | Ready in:

Ingredients

- 3 garlic cloves minced
- 1/2 red onion chopped
- 1/2 red bell pepper chopped
- 1/2 yellow bell pepper diced
- 1 teaspoon cumin
- 2 teaspoons coriander
- juice of 4 lemons
- 1/2 cup olive oil
- 1 jalapeno pepper minced
- 2 cups cooked black beans
- 1 tablespoon cilantro
- 2 oranges peeled and sectioned

Direction

- Combine first nine ingredients in order in large bowl then toss in beans and oranges.
- Mix to coat then season with salt and pepper and serve.

15. Broccoli Orange Salad Recipe

Serving: 12 | Prep: | Cook: 5mins | Ready in:

Ingredients

- Dressing:
- 1 egg
- ¼ c. sugar
- 1 tsp. prepared mustard
- ½ tsp. cornstarch
- 2 Tbsp. water
- 2 Tbsp. cider vinegar
- 2 Tbsp. mayonnaise
- 2 Tbsp. sour cream
- 1 ½ Tbsp. butter
- Combine for the salad:
- 4 c. broccoli flowerets
- 1 c. salted cashews
- 1 c. cubed swiss cheese
- 1 can drained mandarin oranges
- ½ c. chopped craisins/ dried cranberries (can use raisins)
- 6 strips bacon, cooked crisply and crumbled
- ½ c. chopped red onion

Direction

- Combine the egg, sugar, mustard and cornstarch. Whisk until smooth.
- Add the vinegar and water and cook until thickened. Remove from the heat.
- Stir in the mayo, sour cream and butter. Set aside to cool.
- Place salad ingredients in a large bowl and toss.
- Just before serving, add the dressing and toss to coat.

16. Broccoli Orange And Watercress Salad Recipe

Serving: 6 | Prep: | Cook: | Ready in:

Ingredients

- DRESSING:
- 1/4c cider vinegar
- 2T rice vinegar
- 1T olive oil
- 2t sugar
- 1t honey
- 1/4t salt
- 1/8t black pepper, coarsely ground
- SALAD:
- 4c iceburg lettuce, thinley sliced
- 3c small broccoli florets, steamed
- 3c watercress, trimmed
- 2c orange sections, about 4 oranges

Direction

- To save time, steam the broccoli ahead; cover and chill. Section the orange ahead, too.
- To prepare dressing, combine first 7 ingredients in a jar. Cover tightly; shake vigorously.
- To prepare salad, combine lettuce and remaining ingredients in a large bowl. Add dressing; toss well to coat.
- Serving size 1 1/2c; 88 calories; 28% from fat

17. CALIFORNIA AVOCADO MANDARIN SALAD Recipe

Serving: 4 | Prep: | Cook: | Ready in:

Ingredients

- 1 (9 to 10 oz.) pkg. mixed salad greens
- 1 (15 oz.) can mandarin oranges, well-drained
- 1 (6 oz.) pkg. cooked and sliced chicken breast
- 2 thin slices red onion, cut in half and sliced into crescents
- 1/4 cup pecans, toasted
- 1/2 cup prepared bottled light Italian or balsamic vinaigrette dressing
- 2 ripe California avocados, seeded, peeled and cut into chunks

Direction

- In large salad bowl, combine salad greens, mandarin oranges, chicken, onions and pecans.
- In small bowl, combine dressing and 1/2 cup avocado cubes. Mash and blend into dressing.
- Add remaining avocado cubes and dressing to salad. Toss and serve.

18. Chicken Mandarin Salad With Sesame Ginger Dressing Recipe

Serving: 4 | Prep: | Cook: | Ready in:

Ingredients

- 1 cooked chicken breast cut in thin slices (4-6 oz)
- 1/2 head of napa cabbage, washed, dried, and shredded
- 1 small can mandarin oranges
- 1 T almond slivers, toasted
- 1/2 c lowfat or nonfat mayonnaise
- 1/4 c rice wine vinegar
- 3 T honey
- 2 teas lime juice
- 1/2 teas minced garlic
- 1 teas minced ginger (fresh, but half the amount of ginger powder can be substituted in a pinch)
- 1 teas sesame oil

Direction

- Dressing
- Whisk together the mayonnaise, vinegar, honey, sesame oil, lime juice, ginger and garlic. Set aside and let sit for 15 minutes
- In a salad bowl layer the napa, oranges, chickens, and almonds
- Add dressing and toss (you may not need to use all the dressing)
- Enjoy

19. Chicken Salad With Fennel Orange And Raspberries Recipe

Serving: 4 | Prep: | Cook: 25mins | Ready in:

Ingredients

- 1 1/2 lbs boneless, skinless chicken breasts
- 1/2 cup orange juice
- 3 large navel oranges
- 1 fennel bulb, trimmed and coarsely diced
- 8 cups mixed lettuce such as Boston or Bibb, washed and torn into bite-size pieces
- 1 small red onion, thinly sliced
- 1/4 cup raspberries
- Tangy Raspberry-Orange-mustard Dressing:
- 3 Tbs olive oil
- 3 Tbs grainy mustard
- 3 Tbs honey
- 2 Tbs raspberry vinegar
- 1 large navel orange, zest grated and juice squeezed
- salt and freshly ground black pepper, to taste
- Set 4 dinner plates in the refrigerator.

Direction

- In a medium bowl, whisk together all ingredients for the dressing.
- Spoon 2 tablespoons of dressing into a large skillet and set the rest aside. Over medium-low heat, add chicken and orange juice to skillet.
- Bring to a simmer, reduce heat to low and cover the pan.
- Cook chicken for 6 minutes, then turn it over and cook for another 6 minutes.
- Shut off heat, remove lid, and let cool in the pan for 15 minutes.
- Meanwhile, cut off tops and bottoms of remaining 3 oranges with a sharp paring knife; peel the oranges, removing all the white pith, and slice into rounds.
- In a large bowl, toss the fennel and lettuce with all but 2 tablespoons of the reserved dressing.
- Divide the lettuce mixture among the 4 chilled dinner plates.
- Slice the chicken into thin strips.
- Arrange the chicken, orange sections and onion slices on top of lettuce. Drizzle with remaining dressing, sprinkle with raspberries and serve.

20. Chicken And Clementine Orange Salad Recipe

Serving: 2 | Prep: | Cook: | Ready in:

Ingredients

- 6 Ounce Half of a 6-ounce bag mixed baby salad greens
- 2 clementine oranges, peeled and separated into individual segments
- 1 6- or 8-ounce package cooked grilled chicken breast strips or 1-1/2 cups cooked chicken breast strips
- 1/2 Cup chow mein noodles
- 1 Tablespoon orange marmalade
- 3 Tablespoon orange juice
- 1 Tablespoon canola oil
- 1 Tablespoon white wine vinegar
- 1/2 Teaspoon hot Chinese mustard or Dijon-style mustard
- 1 Tablespoon minced scallions
- 1/4 Teaspoon salt
- 1/8 Teaspoon pepper

Direction

- 1. Combine salad greens, orange segments, chicken and chow mein noodles in large salad bowl. Toss gently but well.
- 2. Combine orange marmalade, orange juice, canola oil, vinegar, mustard, scallions, salt and pepper in a small bowl. Stir well to mix. Pour

over salad just before serving; toss gently but well.

- Nutritional Information
- Serving per recipe: 2
- Amt per serving:
- Calories 300
- Carbohydrates 28
- Fat 11 g
- Protein 16 g
- Cholesterol 18 mg
- Dietary Fiber 1.5 g
- Sodium 563 mg

21. Chicken And Mandarin Orange Salad Recipe

Serving: 4 | Prep: | Cook: | Ready in:

Ingredients

- 1 cup mayonnaise
- 1/4 cup lime juice
- 1/4 teaspoon ground nutmeg
- 4 cups cooked chicken cubed
- 11 ounces mandarin oranges
- 1 cup seedless green grape halves
- 3/4 cup celery chopped
- 1/2 cup almonds slivered and toasted

Direction

- Drain oranges then in large bowl combine mayonnaise, lime juice, salt and nutmeg.
- Stir in remaining ingredients and mix well then chill and serve on lettuce leaves.

22. Citrus Avocado Orange And Red Onion Salad Recipe

Serving: 4 | Prep: | Cook: | Ready in:

Ingredients

- spiced sugared pecans
- 1/2 cup unsalted pecan halves
- 3 tbsp granulated sugar
- 2 tsp water
- 1/4 tsp salt
- Generous pinch cayenne pepper
- =====================
- Salad
- 2 seedless oranges
- 3 tbsp olive oil
- 1 tbsp lime juice
- 1/2 tsp salt
- Pinch cayenne pepper
- 1 large, ripe but firm avocado
- 1 head Belgian endive
- 2 paper-thin slices red onion

Direction

- Lightly grease a large piece of foil.
- Place pecans, sugar, water, salt and cayenne in a small frying pan set over medium heat.
- Stir until sugar melts.
- Stir continuously until all the sugar is golden and coats pecans, about 7 minutes.
- Turn onto foil and cool completely.
- Separate into pieces.
- Using a sharp knife, peel 1 orange, removing all white pith.
- Slice orange into very thin rounds.
- Finely grate 1 tsp peel from the remaining orange and squeeze out 2 tbsp. juice.
- Place juice and peel in a small bowl.
- Whisk in oil, lime juice, salt and cayenne.
- Cut avocado in half and remove pit.
- Peel, then slice into thin wedges.
- Separate endive into leaves and arrange on a platter.
- Scatter avocado and orange segments on base of leaves.
- Separate onion into rings, cutting large rings in half.
- Place over salad.
- Drizzle with dressing.
- Sprinkle with pecans.

23. Clementine Vinaigrette Recipe

Serving: 4 | Prep: | Cook: 15mins | Ready in:

Ingredients

- 4 medium clementine, halved
- 6 stalk Fresh green onions, thinly sliced
- 1/4 cup vidalia onion Raw, thinly sliced
- 1/4 cup red bell pepper, Raw, diced
- 5 tbsp Smoky Orange Vinaigrette

Direction

- Peel and remove all pith from the clementines. Cut each section in half and drop them in a bowl to let the juice collect.
- Slice the onions and peppers and add to the bowl. Add the vinaigrette to the mix and toss well. Chill and serve.

24. Cool And Easy Orange And Olive Salad Recipe

Serving: 6 | Prep: | Cook: | Ready in:

Ingredients

- 2 heads romaine lettuce
- 1 bunch watercress or arugula
- 1/2 cup black oil-cured or kalamata olives, pitted, sliced in half
- 1/2 red onion, sliced thinnly
- 2 oranges, peeled and chopped
- Dressing
- 1/2 cup extra virgin olive oil
- salt and black pepper to taste
- 1/4 cup orange juice
- 2 Tbsp. Sherry vinegar

Direction

- Wash and dry the romaine and the watercress. Toss in a large bowl with the other

ingredients. Add freshly ground black pepper to taste (the olives may be salty so don't add any salt at this point). Wisk the dressing ingredients, seasoning it to taste. Slowly pour the dressing over the salad while tossing well to coat all. Be careful not to use too much dressing for the amount of greens. Garnish with very thin slices of orange and orange zest

25. Cucumber Salad With Oranges And Mint Recipe

Serving: 4 | Prep: | Cook: 10mins | Ready in:

Ingredients

- 1 english cucumber,sliced in rounds
- 1(12oz) can mandarin oranges,drained
- 1/4c fresh mint leaves
- 1Tbs sherry vinegar
- 2tsp olive oilsalt and ground pepper

Direction

- In a large bowl, combine cucumber, oranges, mint, vinegar and oil. Toss to combine. Season, to taste, with salt and black pepper.

26. Date And Orange Salad W Feta And Pistachio Recipe

Serving: 6 | Prep: | Cook: | Ready in:

Ingredients

- finely grated zest of 1 organic orange
- 1/2 thinly sliced red onion
- 3 Tbsp white wine vinegar or white balsamic
- 6 large fresh dates
- 4 oranges
- 1 head butter lettuce
- 1/2 tsp salt

- 1/4 tsp paprika
- 1/4 tsp ground cumin
- 1/8 tsp ground coriander
- 1/4 C cilantro
- 1/4 C olive oil
- 1/4 C shelled green pistachios
- 2 ounces feta, thinly sliced
- fresh ground pepper

Direction

- Toss orange zest and onion w/vinegar and chill while preparing salad.
- If dates are hard, cover w/ hot damp towel for 5 minutes or longer until softened. Remove stones and quarter dates lengthwise.
- Section oranges, working over bowl to catch juices.
- Tear lettuce into bite sized pieces.
- Now make vinaigrette by draining vinegar from onion into glass measuring cup and add enough of the orange juice to make 1/4 C.
- Stir in salt, chopped cilantro, spices, and oil.
- Taste for balance and add more vinegar if you want sharper taste.
- Toss the lettuce with orange sections, dates, pistachios, and dressing.
- Mound salad onto a platter, scatter feta overtop
- Grind pepper overtop
- Serve!

27. Dodis Mandarin Orange Onion Salad Recipe

Serving: 6 | Prep: | Cook: |Ready in:

Ingredients

- Head lettuce, torn into bite-size pieces
- fresh spinach, torn into bite-size pieces
- 1 purple onion, sliced
- Canned mandarin oranges, drained (reserve liquid)

- salt
- salad oil
- cider vinegar
- sliced almonds

Direction

- Place 3 parts oil to 1 part vinegar into a jar with tight lid. Add sliced onion, salt and a little re served juice, about 1 T. Shake vigorously, till turns white and thickens. Place equal parts lettuce and spinach in salad bowl. Toss with dressing, including onions. Top salad with oranges and almonds.

28. Easy Salad With Orange Red Onion And Bleu Cheese Vinaigrette Recipe

Serving: 2 | Prep: | Cook: |Ready in:

Ingredients

- Mixed spring greens
- 1/2 red onion
- 1 orange
- Coarsely Chopped pecans or walnuts
- Bleu cheese vinaigrette

Direction

- Put some mixed spring greens into a bowl
- Very thinly slice red onion and add to taste
- Cut orange into bite sized pieces and add to taste
- Sprinkle with nuts to taste
- Top with bleu cheese vinaigrette
- Enjoy!

29. Festive Mandarin Salad Recipe

Serving: 8 | Prep: | Cook: |Ready in:

Ingredients

- mixed greens (enough for large salad bowl)
- One can mandarin oranges
- 1/2 cup sliced almonds
- 1/2 cup dried cranberries
- pinch of poppy seeds
- 1 tbsp olive oil
- 2 tbsp balsamic vinegar
- 1 tbsp juice from mandarin orange can
- 1 tsp sugar
- pinch of salt

Direction

- Put washed greens in salad bowl
- Mix oil, vinegar, juice, sugar and salt. Pour over salad and toss.
- Sprinkle salad with almonds, cranberries and poppy seeds

30. Florida Grapefruit Superfood Salad Recipe

Serving: 4 | Prep: | Cook: 35mins | Ready in:

Ingredients

- • 1 butternut squash
- • 1 cup organic red quinoa
- • 2 Florida grapefruit
- • 1/2 small Napa cabbage
- • 2 cups baby romaine leaves
- • 1 cucumber
- • ½ cup goji berries
- • ½ cup hemp hearts
- • ¼ avocado
- Dressing:• 1 small carrot• 2 green onions• 2 tablespoons white miso• 100 mL fresh Florida grapefruit juice• 1 inch piece of peeled ginger• 1 tablespoon lemon juice• 1 teaspoon salt• 75 mL olive oil• 75 mL canola oil

Direction

- 1. Peel and cut the butternut squash into 1 inch pieces. Blanch in boiling water for about 4 minutes or until just tender. Drain, pat dry and set it aside until ready to use.
- 2. In a small pot, bring 2 cups of lightly salted water to boil. Add the quinoa and turn heat down to medium. Cook the quinoa for 20 minutes or until the quinoa triples in size and becomes tender. Drain and set aside to cool.
- 3. Combine all of the dressing ingredients in a blender and puree on the highest speed for several minutes until very smooth. This can be done a day in advance and held in the refrigerator.
- 4. Using a sharp paring knife, cut the ends off of the Florida grapefruit so it sits flat on the cutting board. Carefully run the paring knife under the peel and trim away all of the pith, leaving just the grapefruit flesh. Slice the grapefruit into 8 even segments.
- 5. Cut the Napa cabbage into quarters and remove the core. Cut the cabbage crosswise into thin shavings. Hold this in a large salad bowl suitable for serving.
- 6. Cut the baby romaine leaves into bite sized pieces and add them to the salad bowl.
- Slice the cucumber lengthwise and remove the seeds. Cut the cucumber on an angle into very thin slices and transfer to the salad bowl.
- 7. Combine the squash, Florida grapefruit slices, hemp hearts, goji berries, avocado and quinoa into the salad bowl and toss liberally with dressing.

31. Fresh Green Salad With Orange Segments And Fat Free Honey Dressing Recipe

Serving: 6 | Prep: | Cook: | Ready in:

Ingredients

- 1/4 cup water
- 1/4 cup white wine vinegar with tarragon

- 1/4 cup honey
- 2 heads butter lettuce, washed and torn
- 1 head radicchio, washed and torn
- 2 oranges, peeled and segmented

Direction

- COMBINE water, vinegar and honey in small shaker or jar; cover. Shake to mix. Arrange lettuce and radicchio on 6 salad plates. Divide orange segments among salad plates; drizzle each with dressing.

32. Fruit Salad (citrus) Recipe

Serving: 0 | Prep: | Cook: | Ready in:

Ingredients

- 3 grapefruit or 4 medium oranges; or 2 oranges and 2 grapefruit
- 1/2 cup French dressing (or mayonnaise)
- lettuce beds

Direction

- Section fruit, pile on lettuce; just before serving pour French dressing or mayonnaise over it.

33. Grated Carrot And Orange Salad Recipe

Serving: 4 | Prep: | Cook: | Ready in:

Ingredients

- 1 tbsp thyme honey
- 1 tbsp orange flower water
- 3 tbsp lemon juice
- 2-3 tbsp orange juice
- 1 tbsp ground of slivered almonds
- ½ tsp salt
- 5 cups carrots, grated

- 2 oranges, each peeled and cut into 8-10 pieces
- 1 tbsp extra virgin olive oil
- 2 tbsp pine nuts
- mint leaves, to garnish (optional)

Direction

- Put the honey in a serving dish, and then mix in the orange flower water and lemon juice and orange juice.
- Add the almonds, salt, carrots and oranges.
- Heat the oil in a small pan and sauté the pine nuts until golden.
- Then remove from pan and add to the salad.
- Toss the salad (if desired, garnish with mint) and serve or chill for later use.

34. Grilled Orange Salad With Balsamic Beet Dressing Recipe

Serving: 4 | Prep: | Cook: 5mins | Ready in:

Ingredients

- 4 cups arugula leaves, rinsed and drained
- 2 large oranges
- 4 oz gorgonzola, crumbled
- 1 c toasted almonds
- No stick cooking spray
- *********************
- 1 med-large beet, peeled
- 1 tbsp balsamic vinegar
- Freshly cracked black pepper
- olive oil

Direction

- Cut each orange into 8 even wedges and remove as many seeds as possible.
- Spray your grilling surface with no stick spray and heat to medium-high heat. Place orange wedges on grill and allow to grill until golden and lightly charred, about 2 minutes. Flip and repeat for second side of wedge.

- Evenly divide arugula among four salad plates. Top with crumbled gorgonzola and toasted almonds. Top with warm, grilled orange wedges.
- Drizzle lightly with balsamic beet dressing and serve.
- **********
- For dressing:
- Preheat oven to 400. Drizzle a sheet of aluminum foil with olive oil and place beet in oil. Fold foil over to make a pocket and seal edges. Allow beet to roast 35-45 minutes or until easily pierced with a knife.
- Allow beet to cool slightly and cut into chunks. Place chunks in blender, along with balsamic vinegar, and puree until smooth.
- Slowly stream in olive oil until desired consistency is reached. Season with fresh cracked black pepper and use immediately, or store in fridge for up to two weeks.

35. Grilled Shrimp And Orange Salad Recipe

Serving: 4 | Prep: | Cook: 5mins | Ready in:

Ingredients

- 2 tablespoon olive oil
- 1 pound large shrimp, peeled and deveined
- ½ teaspoon salt and pepper
- 1 large red bell pepper, seeded and sliced thinly
- 2 large navel oranges, peeled and sectioned
- 1 head romaine lettuce, washed, drained and torn
- *************vinaigrette
- juice of 1 lime
- 2 tablespoon honey
- 1 teaspoon cumin
- salt and pepper to taste
- ¼ cup extra virgin olive oil

Direction

- Season shrimp with salt and pepper and toss in olive oil using a medium mixing bowl.
- Meanwhile heat a grill pan over high heat, about 1 minute.
- Grill shrimp for about 2 to 3 minutes. Remove from pan and slightly cool down.
- Combine shrimp, bell pepper, oranges and lettuce and toss lightly with the dressing. Serve right away.
- ***************VINAIGRETTE: Combine the first 4 ingredients well. Slowly whisk in the oil

36. Honey Lime Mandarin Orange And Grape Parfaits Recipe

Serving: 2 | Prep: | Cook: | Ready in:

Ingredients

- 1/3 c. honey
- 3 Tbl lime juice
- 1 tsp grated lime rind (optional)
- ½ lb. seedless grapes (use either red or green, or a combination for more color in the salad)
- 1 can (11 oz) mandarin oranges in light syrup, drained
- sour cream (for parfait layers)

Direction

- Combine first 3 ingredients well. Place fruit in bowl; drizzle with honey mixture. Stir gently to coat. Cover, chill at least 2 hours.
- Layer fruit and sour cream in glasses to make parfaits.

37. Kumara Sweet Potato And Orange Salad Recipe

Serving: 8 | Prep: | Cook: 15mins | Ready in:

Ingredients

- 1kg sweet potato/Kumara
- Approx 4 oranges
- 400mL Potato Salad
- Approx 3 spring onion shoots (cut up thinly)
- 1 tsp curry powder (Add more if the flavour isn't coming through enough)
- salt and pepper

Direction

- Peel and dice the Sweet Potatoes/Kumara into bite sized chunks
- Boil in salted pot for around 15 minutes or until a knife slides easily through the chunks
- While it's cooking mix together the Potato Salad and Curry Powder and add salt and pepper
- Peel and cut up the Oranges into chunks of the same size
- Drain the Kumara and leave to cool - If you are in a hurry put into the fridge to cool down
- Once cold add the Orange pieces, Spring Onions and the Potato Salad/Curry Powder mixture
- Stir through and serve in a large serving dish

38. Layered Orange Salad Recipe

Serving: 4 | Prep: | Cook: | Ready in:

Ingredients

- 3 oranges, peeled and sliced
- 3 Tbsp. chopped toasted almonds
- 3 Tbsp. halved manzanila (or other green) olives
- 2 Tbsp. chopped fresh parsley
- 1 Tbsp. sherry vinegar or white wine vinegar
- 1 Tbsp. extra virgin olive oil
- 1 Tbsp. honey
- 1 Tbsp. minced red onion

Direction

- Layer orange slices on a platter in rows

- Toss together almonds olives, parsley, vinegar, honey, olive oil and onion in a bowl
- Spoon over oranges
- How simple can this be?!

39. Mandarin Orange Salad Recipe

Serving: 8 | Prep: | Cook: 10mins | Ready in:

Ingredients

- Salad:
- ½ C. sliced almonds
- 6 C. Torn romaine lettuce
- 1 C. Sliced celery
- 3 T. sugar
- 1 - 11 oz. Can of mandarin orange slices, drained
- 3 green onions, sliced
- Dressing:
- ½ C. salad oil
- 2 - 3 T. sugar
- ½ t. ground mustard
- 1/4 C. vinegar
- ½ t. salt
- 1/4 t. garlic powder

Direction

- In a sauce pan over medium heat, cook and stir the almonds and sugar, until the almonds are coated and lightly browned (about 4 minutes). Spread the almonds on a plate or sheet of aluminum foil to cool; gently break apart.
- In a large salad bowl, combine the Romaine lettuce, oranges, celery and onions. Top with the almonds. In a jar with a tight-fitting lid, combine the dressing ingredients; shake well. Pour over the salad and gently toss. Serves 8.
- Notes: I like to add more Lettuce than the recipes states, like 8 to 10 cups. It can easily be stretched to serve more that way too.

- Serve immediately

40. Mandarin Orange Tossed Salad Recipe

Serving: 6 | Prep: | Cook: 10mins | Ready in:

Ingredients

- Salad:
- --------
- 1/2 cup slivered almonds
- 3 T. sugar
- 1/2 head iceberg lettuce
- 1/2 head romaine or leafy lettuce (or try spinach)
- I like the green and red leaf
- 1/2 sweet, red onion, sliced into thin rings
- 1 (11-oz) can mandarin oranges, drained
- --------
- Dressing:
- -------
- 3 T. orange juice
- 3 T. top grade oliveoil
- 2 T. vinegar (your favorite)
- 1 T. sugar or honey
- 1-2 t. poppy seeds, optional
- 1/4 t. salt
- fresh ground pepper

Direction

- In frying pan, heat 3 T. sugar over med-low heat until melted (sugar turns liquid).
- Sprinkle almonds into sugar and stir to coat (almonds clump together).
- Pour onto a greased plate and let cool; separate.
- Tear clean, dry greens into bite-sized pieces.
- Toss greens with sliced onion rings (reserve some for garnish), drained oranges, and cooled, separated candied almonds.
- Shake dressing ingredients together until combined.
- When ready to serve, pour dressing over salad and toss gently to coat.
- Garnish with onion rings.

41. Mandarin Orange/walnut Salad Recipe

Serving: 1 | Prep: | Cook: 15mins | Ready in:

Ingredients

- Romaine hearts and spinach
- mandarin orange slices
- walnuts
- Srawberries, sliced into bite size pieces
- Velveeta crumbles
- Raspberry Vinagerette dressing

Direction

- I make salads individually just because I like making them look nice.....so I take and tear bite size pieces from the romaine hearts and toss with baby spinach. Then toss in about 10 pieces of mandarin orange slices and a handful of strawberry slices. Toss on a handful of walnuts and sprinkle with the cheese. Sprinkle with raspberry vinaigrette dressing to taste. I like to serve the salad with a garnish of tomato basil trinkets....Enjoy!

42. Mandarin Poppy Seed Salad Recipe

Serving: 6 | Prep: | Cook: | Ready in:

Ingredients

- 10-12 oz. pre-washed baby spinach
- 1/3 cup poppy seed dressing
- 1/4 teaspoon ginger
- juice of 1/2 lemon
- 1 11 oz. can mandarin oranges, drained
- 1/2 cup honey-roasted slivered almonds

Direction

- Place spinach in large bowl.
- Combine dressing and ginger.
- Drizzle dressing over spinach.
- Squeeze juice from lemon over salad.
- Just before serving toss to combine.
- Top with oranges and almonds.

43. Mandarin Salad Recipe

Serving: 4 | Prep: | Cook: |Ready in:

Ingredients

- 2 sm cans mandarin oranges,
- 1 head romaine lettuce,
- 1 avocado, Walla Walla onion or Maui onion or green onions
- 1/2 cup sugar (I use a bit less) ,
- 1 tsp. salt,
- 1 tsp grey poupon mustard,
- 1/4 c. white vinegar,
- 2/3 cup oil.

Direction

- Beat 1/2 cup sugar (I use a bit less), 1 tsp. salt, 1 tsp grey poupon mustard, 1/4 c. white vinegar, 2/3 cup oil.
- Grate a little onion into the dressing.
- Add toasted sesame seeds to salad.
- For a change you can substitute strawberries for the oranges and poppy seeds or toasted sliced almonds instead of sesame seeds and use fresh baby spinach instead of the romaine lettuce.
- Enjoy!

44. Mom's Orange Salad (insalata Di Arance) Recipe

Serving: 0 | Prep: | Cook: 10mins |Ready in:

Ingredients

- 4 big oranges
- 2 to 3 scallions cleaned and cut small
- 4 tablespoons olive oil,
- 2 tablespoons water
- crushed red pepper to your taste.
- salt and pepper to taste.

Direction

- Peel oranges, section them and cut into bite sizes.
- Add all ingredients and stir well. Refrigerate before serving.
- Serve with Italian bread.
- Mom added water to the salad so it would make more juice for dipping the bread.

45. Ms Lucys Mandarine Orange Salad Recipe

Serving: 6 | Prep: | Cook: |Ready in:

Ingredients

- 1 bunch of romaine lettuce, broken
- 6 roma tomatoes (which have been air ripened in a hanging wire basket for several day)   T
- his adds flavor to the tomatoes
- OR
- 1-pint grape tomatoes (which taste good year round)
- 4-eggs, boiled and sliced
- 1 can mandarin orange slices, drained
- Poppy Seed Dressing

Direction

- Mix vegetables and mandarin oranges.

- Top with dressing.
- (Doubles well.)

46. Orange & Sage Salad With Goat Cheese Recipe

Serving: 0 | Prep: | Cook: 10mins | Ready in:

Ingredients

- 1-4 oz.log goat cheese, Chavrie Fresh Log
- 6 sage leaves, fresh
- 1 orange
- 1 oz. balsamic vinegar
- 1 oz. olive oil

Direction

- Slice Chavrie Fresh Goat Log into 8-10 slices
- Arrange Goat cheese slices in a single line in a shingled fashion on a rectangle platter
- Zest one Orange and reserve the zest for garnishing
- Remove peel and section each orange into segments
- Drizzle olive oil and vinegar on cheese
- Top with orange segments
- Garnish with orange zest
- Serve at room temperature with sliced baguettes or your favorite crackers

47. Orange Almond Salad Recipe

Serving: 4 | Prep: | Cook: | Ready in:

Ingredients

- 1/4 cup almonds slivered
- 2 green onions chopped
- 1 head romaine lettuce
- 11 ounces mandarin oranges drained
- 1-1/2 cups mushrooms sliced

- Dressing:
- 1 tablespoon granulated sugar
- 1/2 teaspoon dried tarragon
- 1/3 cup vegetable oil
- 1/4 teaspoon salt
- 1/2 teaspoon freshly ground black pepper
- 1/8 teaspoon Tabasco sauce
- 1 egg yolk

Direction

- Shaking constantly toast almonds in skillet over low until golden brown about 5 minutes.
- Wash and dry lettuce then tear into bite size pieces.
- Place lettuce, onions and oranges in large salad bowl.
- Combine all dressing ingredients except yolk.
- Add yolk in thin stream and process until well blended.
- Just before serving toss well and refrigerate leftover dressing.

48. Orange And Fennel Salad Recipe

Serving: 4 | Prep: | Cook: 5mins | Ready in:

Ingredients

- Ingredients:
- 2 medium fennel bulbs, trimmed and thinly sliced(reserve fennel sprigs for garnish)
- 3 Medium heads Belgian endive, trimmed and separated into leaves
- 2 small oranges, peeled and sectioned, each section sliced in half
- 10 small Italian black olives, pitted and halved
- ¼ tsp. salt
- ¼ tsp. Freshly ground black pepper
- 1 Tbs. + 1 tsp. extra virgin olive oil

Direction

- In a large salad bowl, combine fennel, endive, oranges and olives.
- Sprinkle with salt and pepper, drizzle with oil and toss gently.
- Let stand 2 – 3 minutes to allow flavors to blend.
- Divide evenly among 4 salad plates, garnish with fennel sprigs and serve.
- Calories per serving: 104, Fat: 6g, Cholesterol: 0, Sodium: 303mg, Carbohydrate: 13g, Fiber: 4g
- Protein: 2g, Calcium: 85mg

49. Orange And Onion Salad With Toasted Cumin Recipe

Serving: 6 | Prep: | Cook: | Ready in:

Ingredients

- 6 oranges
- 2 red onions sliced thinly in rounds
- 1 1/2 Tbls cumin seeds toasted
- 1 1/2 Tsps coarse black pepper
- 1 1/2 Tbls chopped mint (Mediterranean)
- 6 Tbls Good extra virgin olive oil
- salt to taste
- Fresh mint sprigs and Greek olives to Serve

Direction

- Working over a bowl to catch juice, Slice the Oranges thinly. Holding each slice over the bowl, cut around the slice with a scissors or paring knife to remove the rind. Each slice should end up as a rind less disk.
- Dry toast the cumin seeds until you can see light whiffs of smoke coming from the pan. Try to sprinkle on the salad layers when the seeds are as hot as you can tolerate them.
- Arrange the Onion and Orange slices in layers in a shallow dish. Sprinkle each layer with toasted Cumin seeds, mint, black pepper, Olive Oil, and Salt to taste.

- Pour the Orange Juice left over from the slicing over the finished salad. Leave the salad in a cool place to marinade in for about 2 hours. (It is important to leave it this long but not too much longer before serving.)
- Just before serving scatter the salad with the Mint Sprigs and Greek Olives.

50. Orange Avocado Jicama Salad Recipe

Serving: 4 | Prep: | Cook: | Ready in:

Ingredients

- 1 (5 oz.) bag mixed salad greens, thoroughly washed
- 2 oranges, peeled and sectioned
- 1 avocado, sliced
- 1/4 cup peeled, cubed, jicame (1/2" cubes)
- 6 tbsp cilantro-Lime vinaigrette

Direction

- Toss together first 4 ingredients in a large bowl.
- Serve immediately with Cilantro-Lime Vinaigrette.

51. Orange Blush Lobster Salad Recipe

Serving: 12 | Prep: | Cook: 15mins | Ready in:

Ingredients

- 2 pounds cooked lobster meat*, cut into 1-inch pieces
- 3 cups cantaloupe balls
- 1 diced papaya (about 1¼ pounds), peeled, seeded and cut into ½-inch dice

- 6 diced plum tomatoes (about 2 cups), seeded and cut into ¼-inch dice
- 1 Tablespoon freshly minced ginger
- ¼ cup fresh orange juice
- 2 Tablespoons red-wine vinegar
- 1 teaspoon dijon-style mustard
- To taste salt and black pepper
- ½ cup extra-virgin olive oil
- 1 teaspoon finely grated orange zest
- ¼ cup freshly snipped chives
- 2 heads radicchio, leaves washed and patted dry, for garnish

Direction

- Place the lobster meat, cantaloupe, papaya, tomatoes and ginger in a large bowl. Gently fold together with a rubber spatula. Set aside.
- In a small bowl, combine the orange juice, vinegar, mustard, salt and pepper. Whisking constantly, slowly drizzle in the olive oil. Continue whisking until the mixture has thickened slightly. Stir in orange zest (makes ¾ cup).
- Shortly before serving, toss ½ cup of the dressing with the chives and lobster mixture. Serve on a decorative platter surrounded by radicchio leaves, or place serving portions inside the leaves.
- Serve remaining dressing on the side or reserve for future use.
- *If fresh lobster meat is unavailable, a frozen brand can be found in many supermarkets. If you want to cook your own you'll need six lobsters, about 1½ pounds each.

52. Orange Chicken Salad Recipe

Serving: 4 | Prep: | Cook: 30mins | Ready in:

Ingredients

- 2 seedless oranges
- 2 cups chicken stock
- 1 cup long grain rice

- 1/2 cup extra virgin olive oil
- 1/4 cup orange juice
- 2 teaspoons Dijon mustard
- 1 pound cooked chicken diced
- 1/2 cup cashews lightly toasted
- 3 tablespoons chopped fresh chives
- salt and freshly ground pepper to taste

Direction

- Peel one of the oranges being careful to remove only the thin orange part of the peel leaving the white pith behind.
- Combine the orange peel, chicken stock and rice in a pot and bring to a boil over moderate heat.
- Reduce heat and simmer covered for 15 minutes.
- Remove from heat and let stand covered for 10 minutes.
- Meanwhile whisk together olive oil, orange juice and Dijon mustard then set aside.
- Remove and discard the orange zest from the rice.
- Transfer rice to a serving bowl and toss with half of the dressing.
- Cool to room temperature or chill in the refrigerator.
- Completely peel both oranges and divide into segments.
- Immediately before serving toss rice with the remaining dressing.
- Add chicken, cashews and chives then toss well to combine.
- Adjust seasoning with salt and pepper and garnish with orange segments.

53. Orange Mint Salad Recipe

Serving: 4 | Prep: | Cook: | Ready in:

Ingredients

- SALAD:
- 1 orange, peeled & cut into chunks

- 3 c. chopped romaine lettuce
- 1/4 c. chopped walnuts
- 1/2 c. chopped red onions
- 2 T. chopped fresh mint
- DRESSING:
- 3 T. extra-virgin olive oil
- 1 T. balsamic vinegar
- 1 T. orange juice
- 1 garlic clove, crushed
- salt and pepper to taste

Direction

- Mix all salad ingredients in a serving bowl.
- Whisk dressing ingredients in a separate bowl.
- Then toss with salad.

54. Orange Onion Salad Recipe

Serving: 2 | Prep: | Cook: | Ready in:

Ingredients

- 1 tbsp olive oil
- 2 tsp white wine vinegar
- 3/4 tsp sugar
- 1/8 to 1/4 tsp ground cumin
- dash each of paprika, curry powder, cinnamon and pepper
- 2 small navel oranges, peeled and sliced
- 2 slices red onion, quartered
- 1 tbsp minced fresh cilantro

Direction

- Combine oil, vinegar, sugar, cumin, paprika, curry, cinnamon, and pepper
- Place oranges and onion in a shallow bowl
- Drizzle with dressing, toss gently to coat
- Sprinkle with cilantro

55. Orange Pear Spinach Salad Recipe

Serving: 8 | Prep: | Cook: | Ready in:

Ingredients

- 2 medium red or yellow pears
- lemon juice
- 4 cups fresh spinach leaves
- 4 cups leaf lettuce
- 3 oranges peeled halved and sectioned
- Vinaigrette:
- 1/4 cup olive oil
- 1/4 cup balsamic vinegar
- 2 tablespoons sugar
- 1 teaspoon snipped fresh basil crushed
- 1 teaspoon snipped fresh thyme crushed
- 1/2 teaspoon snipped fresh marjoram crushed

Direction

- Slice pears then brush cut edges with lemon juice.
- On a serving platter arrange spinach and lettuce then top with orange and pear slices.
- Combine all dressing ingredients in a jar then cover and shake well to mix.
- Before serving add dressing to greens then toss to coat.

56. Orange Poppy Seed Salad Recipe

Serving: 6 | Prep: | Cook: | Ready in:

Ingredients

- 1 egg white
- 1/4 cup sugar
- 1 cup almonds, sliced
- 1 head bibb lettuce, torn
- 11 ounces mandarin orange, canned
- 16 ounces strawberries, sliced
- 1 green onion, chopped

- 3/4 cup olive oil
- 1/4 cup red wine vinegar
- 1 teaspoon orange rind, grated
- 1 tablespoon orange juice
- 1/2 teaspoon poppy seeds
- 1/8 teaspoon salt

Direction

- Beat egg white at high speed with an electric mixer until foamy. Add sugar, 1 tbsp. at a time, beating 2 to 4 minutes or until stiff peaks form and sugar dissolves. Fold in almonds.
- Melt butter in a 9 inch square pan in a 325 F oven. Add almonds to pan and bake, stirring every 5 minutes, for 20 - 25 minutes or until lightly browned and dry . Cool in pan on a wire rack.
- Toss together Bibb lettuce and next 4 ingredients in a large bowl.
- Whisk together oil and balance of ingredients; drizzle half over salad, tossing gently.
- Sprinkle with sugared almonds and serve immediately with remaining dressing.

57. Orange Radish Salad Recipe

Serving: 4 | Prep: | Cook: |Ready in:

Ingredients

- 2 cups seedless orange sections
- 1 cup grated radishes
- 1 tablespoon cilantro chopped
- 1/4 cup fresh orange juice
- 1 tablespoon powdered sugar
- 1/8 teaspoon salt

Direction

- Combine all ingredients in a medium bowl and stir.
- Cover and let stand at room temperature for 1 hour before serving.

58. Orange Romaine Salad Recipe

Serving: 4 | Prep: | Cook: 10mins |Ready in:

Ingredients

- Romaine or boston lettuce, you could use anything really
- 3 mandarin oranges, or use navel
- 2 celery stalks, sliced fine
- 1/2 cup toasted sliced almonds
- 2-3 green onions, chopped
- Dressing:
- 2 tbsp. orange juice
- 1 tbsp. white vinegar
- 1 tbsp. olive oil
- 1/4 tsp. salt
- fresh ground pepper
- 3 tsp sugar

Direction

- Divide your lettuce into serving/salad bowls. Separate the orange sections and arrange on top of lettuce. Sprinkle the celery, almonds and green onions over top.
- Mix up your dressing by whisking the orange juice, vinegar, olive oil, salt, pepper and sugar together in a little bowl. Serve on the side.
- Enjoy!

59. Orange Salad Cups Recipe

Serving: 6 | Prep: | Cook: |Ready in:

Ingredients

- 3 large oranges
- 1 large red apple
- 1/3 cup diced celery
- 3 Tbsp mayonnaise
- ½ tsp salt
- ½ tsp sugar

- 6 walnut or pecan halves

Direction

- Cut each orange in half. If you are artistic, you may cut them with zigzag edges. (I am not artistic; I would probably cut myself or ruin my orange cups.)
- Cut the pulp out of the orange halves with a grapefruit knife, then cut pulp into small pieces and put them in a small bowl.
- Save your empty orange halves. They are your cups for the salad.
- Core and dice the unpeeled red apple.
- Combine orange pulp, diced apple and celery.
- Mix the mayonnaise together with the salt and sugar, then mix into the fruit and celery mixture.
- Divide the mixture between the orange cups.
- Top each cup with a nut half.
- Serve chilled. You may hold the cups in the refrigerator up to 2 hours before serving.

60. Orange Salad Dressing Recipe

Serving: 8 | Prep: | Cook: |Ready in:

Ingredients

- 2 Tbls   olive oil
- 1 Tbl   white wine vinegar
- 1 Tbl   honey
- 2 Tbl   orange juice (fresh squeezed)
- 1/2 Tbl   Dijon mustard
- 1 clove   Minced garlic
- 1/2 tsp (each) salt & pepper

Direction

- Mix well :)

61. Orange Salad With Cinnamon Recipe

Serving: 4 | Prep: | Cook: 5mins |Ready in:

Ingredients

- 4 oranges, peeled and sliced
- 1 tbsp. sugar
- 1/2 tsp. cinnamon
- 1/2 cup walnuts, toasted and chopped
- some fresh basil chopped

Direction

- Mix all ingredients and serve.

62. Orange Spinach Salad Recipe

Serving: 4 | Prep: | Cook: |Ready in:

Ingredients

- 10 oz baby spinach
- 2 small cans mandarin orange segments
- 1/3 c. slivered almonds, toasted
- 2 green onions, chopped
- vinaigrette dressing of your choice, to taste

Direction

- In a large bowl; combine spinach, oranges, almonds and onions. Add vinaigrette dressing to taste and toss.

63. Orange Vinagrette Salad Recipe

Serving: 5 | Prep: | Cook: |Ready in:

Ingredients

- 1 small bag of crisp romaine salad
- 1 container of cherry tomatoes

- 1 medium avacado cup up into slices
- vinaigrette:
- 1 large orange
- 1/2 cup apple cider vinegar
- 1/2 cup (or less) olive oil
- 1/2 tsp basil
- 2 tbs honey

Direction

- In a blender, puree orange pulp.
- Transfer to jar and add all other vinaigrette ingredients.
- Shake and your dressing is done!
- Toss all ingredients together in a salad bowl and serve for a healthy meal.

64. Orange Vinaigrette Chicken Salad Recipe

Serving: 6 | Prep: | Cook: 20mins | Ready in:

Ingredients

- 1 head romaine lettuce: cleaned, dried and chopped
- 1 pound chicken breast halves, boneless and skinless
- 1 cup baby carrots, chopped
- 1 cup fresh broccoli, chopped
- 1 (11 oz) can mandarin oranges, liquid removed
- 1/2 cup white wine vinegar
- 4 tbsp garlic and herb seasoning blend (salt-free)
- 1 1/2 tbsp white sugar
- 1/2 cup orange juice
- 1/4 cup olive oil

Direction

- Preheat grill at a medium-high heat.
- Combine vinegar, seasoning blend, sugar, orange juice, and olive oil in a bowl, then place about 1/2 cup aside for basting.

- Oil the grill grate, lightly, and grill the chicken for 6-8 minutes on both sides, (or until the juices run clear), basting often with the left over portion of dressing. When cooled, cut into strips. Discard the remaining basting sauce.
- In a large bowl, combine the lettuce, carrots, broccoli and oranges. Add the chicken strips to the top of the salad and drizzle with left over dressing to serve.

65. Orange And Fennel Salad Recipe

Serving: 4 | Prep: | Cook: | Ready in:

Ingredients

- 1 large fennel bulb, trimmed
- 2 medium oranges, peeled and trimmed of pith and segmented or sliced
- (blood oranges would add a brilliant colour contrast)
- 1 tablespoon extra virgin olive oil
- 1 teaspoon poppyseeds
- (Optional) shaved parmigiano-Reggiano

Direction

- Slice the fennel bulb
- Slice or segment the oranges
- Place all ingredients on a serving platter
- Drizzle with the olive oil
- Top with poppy seeds
- Allow to rest for 5 minutes or more to allow the flavours to blend
- Serve at room temperature
- Note: Reserve the leaves for garnish on the platter or for use in another dish. They can also be dried and stored for later use

66. Orange Cranberry Pecan Mixed Green Salad Recipe

Serving: 6 | Prep: | Cook: 30mins | Ready in:

Ingredients

- 1 cup and 3 tablespoons orange juice
- 3 1/2 tablespoons olive oil
- 3 oranges (remove peel and segment)
- 6 tablespoons dried cranberries
- 6 cups mixed baby greens
- 3/4 cups toasted pecans
- 1 tablespoon grated orange peel
- 2 tablespoons white wine vinegar

Direction

- Bring 1 (one) cup of orange juice to a light simmer in a saucepan. Remove from heat source.
- Stir in your dried cranberries, let it sit until softened (takes approximately 30 minutes).
- Drain this and throw away the soaking juice.
- Whisk up orange peel, oil, vinegar, and your remaining 3 tablespoons of orange juice in a small bowl. Mix in the cranberries.
- Season the dressing with salt and pepper to taste.
- Put your greens in a good-sized bowl and toss with about 2/3 of the dressing you made.
- Divvy up the greens into 6-8 bowls then put in your orange segments and toss with remaining dressing.
- Finally top off each salad with orange segments and your roasted pecans!

67. Orange Tomato Salad Recipe

Serving: 1 | Prep: | Cook: | Ready in:

Ingredients

- 2 small tomatoes
- 1 medium carrot
- 1 orange
- Some coriander leaves
- For the dressing:
- 1 tbsp mustard oil/olive oil
- 2 tbsp lime juice
- 1 tsp green chilly sauce
- 1 tsp soya sauce
- 1 tsp red pepper sauce

Direction

- Cut tomatoes, carrot and orange into small pieces (remove seeds and outer skin of the orange first).
- Just mix all the ingredients for the dressing together and pour over the salad ingredients.
- Sprinkle some coriander and mix well.

68. Orange Almond Asian Salad Recipe

Serving: 6 | Prep: | Cook: 12mins | Ready in:

Ingredients

- Dressing:
- 1/3 C sugar
- 1/2 C vegetable oil
- 1/4 C Distilled vinegar
- 2 Tbl. soy sauce
- 1/2 tsp. ground ginger
- Salad:
- 1 head bok choy or romaine lettuce, rinsed
- 1 bunch green onions
- 2 packages (3 ounces each) ramen noodles
- 4 ounces slivered almonds
- 2 ounces sesame seeds
- 1 can (11 ounces) mandarin oranges, drained

Direction

- Combine the dressing ingredients in a saucepan; boil for 1 minute; let cool.

- Cut off the root end of the bok choy. Separate the leaves; rinse, drain and tear into bitesize pieces.
- Chop the green onions. Place in a large bowl.
- Break the uncooked noodles into a skillet (discard or save the noodle seasoning packets to use in a recipe calling for a bouillon cube.)
- Add the nuts and seeds.
- Cook, stirring, over medium heat 10 minutes or until brown.
- Toss with all other ingredients.

69. Paprika Chicken And Orange Salad Recipe

Serving: 4 | Prep: | Cook: 20mins | Ready in:

Ingredients

- 4 boneless skinless chicken breast halves
- 1/2 teaspoon paprika
- 1/4 teaspoon salt
- 1 tablespoon extra virgin olive oil
- 8 cups mixed salad greens
- 4 small oranges peeled and segmented
- 1 medium red onion very thinly sliced
- Dressing:
- 3 tablespoons spanish olive oil
- 3 tablespoons sherry vinegar
- 1/4 teaspoon salt
- 1/8 teaspoon freshly ground black pepper

Direction

- Sprinkle chicken with paprika and salt.
- Heat oil in a large skillet over medium low heat.
- Add chicken and cook 8 minutes turning twice.
- Remove chicken to a plate and cool.
- Combine all dressing ingredients and mix well then pour dressing into skillet.
- Stir to remove brown bits then strain into a measuring cup.

- Add enough water to measure 1/3 cup then reserve.
- To serve cut each breast diagonally into 1" slices.
- Arrange greens on 4 dinner plates then top with orange segments and red onion rings.
- Fan one chicken breast on each salad then drizzle with reserved sherry vinegar mixture.

70. Pasta And Avocado Salad Recipe

Serving: 4 | Prep: | Cook: 35mins | Ready in:

Ingredients

- 2 cups pasta shapes (mixture of shells and penne pasta but any shape will do)
- 3 tbsps mayonnaise
- 2 tsps tahini (sesame paste)
- 1 orange
- 1/2 medium red pepper (green or yellow will do also)
- 1 medium avocado
- pumpkin seeds to garnish (optional)

Direction

- 1. Cook pasta according to directions and leave to cool.
- 2. Mix together the mayonnaise and tahini.
- 3. Chop the orange into small pieces, retaining any juice.
- 4. Chop the pepper
- 5. Stir the mayo mixture and, pepper and orange (plus juice) into the cooled pasta.
- 6. Just before serving, cube the avocado and stir in carefully so not to mash it.
- 7. Garnish with pumpkin seeds.

71. Pina Colada Chicken Salad Recipe

Serving: 4 | Prep: | Cook: 20mins | Ready in:

Ingredients

- romaine lettuce,
- 3-4 Grilled chicken breast cubed
- 1 can mandarin oranges
- .5 oz shaved coconut
- 1 small package macadamia nuts (crushed)
- 1 can pineapple chunks
- 3/4 cup crumbled feta cheese (optional)
- *dressing
- 1/2 cup plus 2 TBSP sugar
- 1/3 cup mr. & mrs. T's pina colada drink mix
- 1/3 cup rice or apple cider vinegar- rice will make it more mild or
- apple cider will make it stronger tasting
- 1/2 tsp. ginger powder
- 1 tsp. dry mustard
- 1/2 tsp. salt
- 1 1/4 cup vegetable oil

Direction

- Toss all of the ingredients together in a large bowl or layer on a platter. Serve with Pina Colada Vinaigrette dressing.
- *Dressing
- In a blender combine all ingredients except the oil. Blend well until light & frothy. With the blender still on, slowly add oil in a steady stream. Keep blending until the dressing is emulsified & thickened.

72. Pina Colada Fruit Salad

Serving: 0 | Prep: | Cook: | Ready in:

Ingredients

- 6 eaches fresh strawberries, hulled and sliced
- 1 peach, sliced
- 1 banana, sliced
- ½ cup watermelon chunks
- ½ cup fresh blueberries
- ½ cup fresh pineapple chunks
- ¼ cup pina colada mix

Direction

- Mix the strawberries, peach, banana, watermelon, blueberries, and pineapple together in a large bowl. Drizzle the pina colada mix over the fruit; stir until evenly coated.

73. Pomegranate Papaya Kiwi Orange Salad Recipe

Serving: 6 | Prep: | Cook: | Ready in:

Ingredients

- 1 1/2 tsp white wine vinegar
- 1/4 tsp salt
- 1/8 tsp pepper
- 1/8 tsp crushed red pepper flakes
- 1/4 cup olive oil
- 1 1/2 quarts mixed salad greens
- 2 oranges, peeled and sliced
- 2 medium papayas, peeled and sliced
- 4 kiwis, peeled and sliced
- 1 medium pomegranate, seeded (about 3/4 cup)

Direction

- Dressing: combine vinegar and next 3 ingredients, whisk in oil.
- Toss greens with 2 1/2 tbsp. dressing arrange on a serving platter
- Alternate orange, papaya and kiwi slices over greens
- Drizzle with remaining dressing. Sprinkle with pomegranate seeds.

74. Poppy Seed Spinach Salad With Grapefruit And Oranges Recipe

Serving: 4 | Prep: | Cook: |Ready in:

Ingredients

- 4 cups cleaned spinach torn into bite size pieces
- 1 ruby red grapefruit peeled and sectioned
- 1 navel orange peeled and sectioned
- 1/2 red onion sliced and separated into rings
- 1/4 cup sliced almonds
- 1/2 cup bottled poppy seed dressing

Direction

- Arrange spinach on salad plates and fan orange and grapefruit sections on top.
- Arrange rings of onion on top then sprinkle with almonds and pour dressing over top.
- Mix gently to combine then serve immediately.

75. Pork TenderloinAnd Wild Rice Salad With Orange Dressing Recipe

Serving: 4 | Prep: | Cook: 30mins |Ready in:

Ingredients

- 6 ounce package wild rice
- nonstick cooking spray
- 1 pound pork tenderloin
- 1 cup sliced green onions
- 1 cup seedless green grapes halved
- 1/2 cup chopped pecans toasted
- 1 tablespoon grated orange peel
- 1 cup fresh orange juice
- 1/3 cup sherry vinegar
- 1/4 teaspoon salt
- 1/8 teaspoon black pepper

- 7 red leaf lettuce leaves

Direction

- Cook rice according to package directions omitting salt then drain.
- Preheat oven to 375,
- Place a large skillet coated with non-stick cooking spray over medium high heat until hot.
- Add pork then cook until lightly browned on all sides.
- Place in a rectangular baking dish coated with non-stick cooking spray then bake 30 minutes.
- Cool completely then cut into thick strips.
- Combine pork, wild rice, green onions, grape halves and pecans in a large bowl.
- Combine orange peel, juice, vinegar, salt and pepper in a small bowl and stir with a whisk.
- Pour over pork and toss to coat then serve salad at room temperature on lettuce lined plates.

76. Raspberry Orange Vinaigrette With Wild Rice Salad Recipe

Serving: 6 | Prep: | Cook: 20mins |Ready in:

Ingredients

- 1-1/3 cups sun dried apricots cut in fourths
- 1-1/2 cups sun dried peaches chopped
- 1-1/2 cups dried cranberries
- 3/4 cup orange flavored liqueur
- 1-1/2 cups wild rice well rinsed
- 6-3/4 cups chicken broth divided use
- 1 teaspoon kosher salt
- 2 cups long grain white rice
- 1/2 cup loosely packed fresh chervil leaves coarsely chopped
- Vinaigrette:
- 1/3 cup raspberry vinegar
- 1/2 teaspoon kosher salt
- 1/2 cup canola oil

- 1 heaping tablespoon Dijon mustard
- 1 teaspoon freshly ground black pepper
- 1/2 cup fresh raspberries

Direction

- In medium bowl, combine apricots, peaches, cranberries and liqueur.
- Stir with wooden spoon to coat fruit and liqueur.
- Cover with plastic wrap and set aside at least 2 hours stirring mixture from time to time.
- In large saucepan combine wild rice, 3-3/4 cups broth and salt.
- Bring to boil on medium high heat then cover and reduce to simmer on low heat.
- Cook 55 minutes then set pan aside covered to cool.
- Meanwhile in large saucepan combine long grain rice, remaining broth and salt.
- Bring to boil on high heat then cover and reduce heat to low and cook 15 minutes.
- Set pot aside covered to cool.
- Drain fruits in fine strainer set over mixing bowl.
- Press fruits with back of wooden spoon to extract liqueur then reserve liquid for vinaigrette.
- In large glass salad bowl combine two varieties of rice, fruit and chervil then set aside.
- To reserved liqueur add vinegar and salt then stir until salt dissolves.
- Add oil, mustard and several turns of pepper then whisk until ingredients are blended.
- In small bowl crush raspberries with fork then add to vinaigrette mixture and stir gently.
- Pour vinaigrette over rice salad and toss to combine.
- Taste and add more salt and pepper if needed.
- Cover lightly with plastic wrap and refrigerate at least 2 hours then toss again before serving.
- Serve well chilled.

77. Red Onion Orange Salad Recipe

Serving: 8 | Prep: | Cook: | Ready in:

Ingredients

- 6 sweet, ripe medium oranges, peeled
- 1 small red onion, sliced finely
- 1/4 cup white balsamic vinegar
- 1/2 cup extra-virgin olive oil
- salt & freshly ground black pepper
- 1.5 ounces organic raisins
- 20 black olives, pitted and halved
- 2 tablespoons sunflower seeds
- 2 tablespoons almonds, blanched and sliced thinly

Direction

- Boil some water and soak raisins in the hot water for 20 minutes, removing from heat. Drain and set aside.
- Remove the white pith from the oranges and cut the fruit crosswise into 1/4 inch slices.
- Arrange the oranges on a serving platter and scatter over the sliced red onion.
- In a small bowl, whisk together the vinegar, olive oil, salt and pepper.
- Drizzle this dressing over the onions and oranges.
- Sprinkle with the raisins, olives, sunflower seeds, and almonds.
- Serve chilled.

78. Roasted Beet Salad W Orange Amp Beet Greens Recipe

Serving: 6 | Prep: | Cook: 45mins | Ready in:

Ingredients

- 6 medium beets with beet greens attached (combination of red and yellow works great too! Check with your local farmer.)

- 2 large oranges (segments cut out and reserved)
- 1 small sweet onion, cut through root end into thin wedges
- 1/3 cup red wine vinegar
- 1/4 cup extra-virgin olive oil
- 2 garlic cloves, minced
- 1/2 teaspoon grated orange peel
- salt to taste

Direction

- Preheat oven to 300
- Cut beet greens from beets, and wash both under cold water.
- Place beets in a bowl, lightly oil and salt them, toss to coat.
- In a deep baking dish, place beets inside, pour enough water in the dish so that it comes up about 1/4 of the beet.
- Cover tightly with foil, and bake for 45 min, or until tender with a knife.
- Cook beet greens in large saucepan of salted boiling water just until tender, about 2 minutes. Drain. Cool. Squeeze greens to remove excess moisture.
- Once beets are done, let cool, and remove the skin with a cloth rag, and slice into quarters.
- Combine beet greens, quartered beets, orange segments, and onion in large bowl.
- In a smaller bowl, whisk together the red wine vinegar, EVOO, garlic, and grated orange peel.
- Dress beets with dressing, and serve

79. Roasted Beets And Roots Salad With Oranges Recipe

Serving: 4 | Prep: | Cook: 60mins | Ready in:

Ingredients

- 6 beets
- 6 carrots
- 6 parsnips
- 2 garlic bulbs

- 2 large red onions
- 4-5 spoons olive oil
- salt and pepper
- 2 tsp honey
- 2 tsp balsamic vinegar
- 3 oranges
- 1 tbsp diced mint

Direction

- Peel and chop vegetables in small cubes. Set onions on the side. Mix the rest of the veggies with salt and pepper and olive oil. You can keep the garlic in peel and squeeze them out once they are roasted, or peel them ahead. Roast at 425F for 35 minutes. Add the peeled and cut onions and roast another 15 minutes. Mix all the rest in a bowl with the roasted vegetables and serve.

80. Roasted Orange Pepper Salad Dressing Recipe

Serving: 8 | Prep: | Cook: 20mins | Ready in:

Ingredients

- 1 orange, Yellow or red pepper
- 3/4t sugar
- 1t shallot, finely diced
- generous salt and pepper
- 1t Dijon mustard
- 1/4C apple cider vinegar
- 1/3C olive oil

Direction

- Roast the pepper. To roast the pepper put it on a baking sheet under the broiler and broil, turning every 3-5 minutes until all sides are blistered. Place in a sealed Ziploc bag and allow to cool until you can handle it - but at least 10 minutes. (This will create a steam pocket and will make it easier to peel.)

- Peel, de-seed and core the pepper and put in a food processor and blend until smooth. Add remaining ingredients and process until blended and uniform.

81. Romaine Salad With Orange Vinaigrette Recipe

Serving: 6 | Prep: | Cook: |Ready in:

Ingredients

- SALAD
- 1/2 package (10 oz.) fresh romaine lettuce leaves
- 1/2 cup matchstick carrots
- 1/2 medium red delicious apple, cut in large chunks
- 1/2 cup seedless red grapes
- 1/2 cup mandarin oranges, drained
- 1/4 cup pecan pieces
- ORANGE vinaigrette
- 1/4 cup sweet orange marmalade
- 2 tbsp white wine vinegar
- 1 tbsp olive oil
- 1/8 teaspoon ground ginger

Direction

- Place first four salad ingredients in large bowl, toss gently.
- Arrange oranges on top of salad mixture.
- Cover and refrigerate until serving time.
- Combine all ingredients for Orange Vinaigrette, set aside.
- Drizzle with Orange Vinaigrette, top with pecans, and toss gently before serving.

82. Russian Style Carrot And Orange Salad Recipe

Serving: 1 | Prep: | Cook: |Ready in:

Ingredients

- 2-3 carrots (preferably small ones), shredded or grated fine
- 1 orange
- 2 tbsp of sour cream or vanilla yogurt

Direction

- Put carrots in a bowl
- Peel the orange and separate the segments. Cut them in small pieces, about 1 cm
- Add orange pieces to the bowl, add sour cream or yogurt, mix it all with the carrots
- If you are using sour cream, you can add a bit of sugar
- You can also add soaked raisins or crushed nuts if you like

83. SPINACH SALAD WITH ORANGE VINAIGRETTE Recipe

Serving: 4 | Prep: | Cook: 20mins |Ready in:

Ingredients

- • 6 slices prosciutto
- • 2 oranges, zested
- • 2 small oranges, juiced or 1 large orange, juiced
- • 2 tablespoons balsamic vinegar
- • 2 tablespoons honey
- • 1 clove garlic, peeled
- • 3/4 teaspoon salt
- • 3/4 teaspoon freshly ground black pepper
- • 3/4 cup extra-virgin olive oil
- • 10 to 12 ounces pre-washed spinach

Direction

- Directions
- Preheat the oven to 350 degrees F.
- Place the prosciutto slices on a baking sheet and bake until just crisp, about 10 minutes. Let

cool. Crumble the prosciutto slices into a container and store in the refrigerator.

- In a blender, combine the orange zest, orange juice, balsamic vinegar, honey, garlic, salt, and pepper. Blend until smooth. With the blender running, add the olive oil in a steady stream until combined. Transfer to a container and store in the refrigerator.
- To serve, put the spinach in a large bowl. Toss with enough of the vinaigrette to coat the spinach. Sprinkle with the crisp prosciutto crumbles, toss again, and serve.

84. Salad With Orange Recipe

Serving: 2 | Prep: | Cook: | Ready in:

Ingredients

- 2 ripe sweet flesh oranges peeled.
- 3 spring onions white + green sliced.
- 2 cloves garlic sliced.
- 1 tbs dill chopped.
- 1 c parsley chopped.
- 1 handfull mint leaves.
- 1 celery stalk cut in 4 lengthwise, chopped.
- 1 lettuce torn in pieces.
- 2 firm tomatoes sliced.
- 1 red pepper chopped.
- 10 black olives without stones.
- 5 tbs olive oil.
- 3 tbs balsamic vinegar.
- juice of 1/2 lemon.
- 6 drops tabasco.
- 1 tbs mustard.
- 1 tbs honey.
- 1 ts sweet paprika.
- salt and pepper to taste.

Direction

- Put olive oil, balsamic, lemon juice, honey and mustard in a jar with lid on and shake till well mixed, set aside and shake again before use.

- Clean oranges from all white parts and seeds, part and put in a big bowl.
- Add onion, garlic, dill, lettuce, tomatoes, red pepper, olives, celery and parsley, mix well and add salt and pepper to taste, mix again.
- Add dressing and mix, sprinkle with paprika and top with mint leaves.

85. Spinach Salad With Orange Cream Dressing Recipe

Serving: 10 | Prep: | Cook: 8mins | Ready in:

Ingredients

- 1 large bag fresh spinach
- 2 cups roasted pine nuts (or sub walnut, pecan, etc)
- 10-12 strips pepper bacon
- 1 1/2 cups mayo or veganaise
- 1/3 container frozen concentrated orange juice

Direction

- Fry bacon until crisp then set aside till cool.
- Place fresh spinach, pine nuts, and crumbled bacon together in large bowl.
- In a separate bowl place mayo and frozen orange juice concentrate together until well mixed.
- Serve dressing over salad when ready to eat and not before or the citric acid will wilt the spinach.
- May be good with fresh crumbled blue or gorgonzola cheese too.

86. Spinach Salad With Oranges And Feta Cheese Recipe

Serving: 3 | Prep: | Cook: | Ready in:

Ingredients

- 1 large Naval orange
- 1/4 cup Citrus vinaigrette (approximately; see separate recipe)
- 8 cups spinach leaves torn
- 2 scallions very thinly sliced
- 1/3 cup feta cheese finely crumbled
- 16 kalamata olives

Direction

- Peel the orange and separate the sections. Remove any course membranes, then cut each section in half and place in a small bowl. Toss with a teaspoon or so for dressing, just enough to coat them lightly.
- Place the spinach and scallions in a large salad bowl. Just before serving, toss with approximately ¼ cup dressing, just enough to coat the leaves.
- Divide the spinach onto 4 salad plates. Sprinkle on the oranges, feta cheese, and olives. Serve immediately.

87. Spinach And Orange Salad Recipe

Serving: 6 | Prep: | Cook: 30mins | Ready in:

Ingredients

- 3/4 lb fresh spinach, torn into bite-size pieces
- 3 medium oranges, peeled, sectioned, and seeded
- 1 medium red onion, sliced and separated into rings
- 1/4-1/3 cup French dressing (try one from this site)

Direction

- Wash spinach thoroughly and allow to dry (use a salad spinner, if you have one).
- Combine spinach, orange sections, and sliced onion in a large salad bowl, tossing well.

- Drizzle dressing over spinach mixture; toss gently.

88. Strawberry Clementine Salad Recipe

Serving: 6 | Prep: | Cook: 15mins | Ready in:

Ingredients

- 5 clementine tangerines
- 2 nectarines
- 2cups fresh strawberries
- 1/4 cup lemon juice
- 3 tbsp agave nectar
- 1 tsp Splenda for Baking
- 1/2 tsp of ground ginger
- Pinch of salt

Direction

- In a large glass bowl combine the following:
- Peel and halve the Clementines then pull apart each section.
- Pit then slice the nectarines and dice.
- Quarter the strawberries.
- In a cup combine the lemon juice, Agave Nectar, ginger, Splenda and salt. Pour over fruit then toss. Chill and serve.

89. Strawberry Orange Chicken Salad Recipe

Serving: 4 | Prep: | Cook: | Ready in:

Ingredients

- 2 cups fresh spinach torn
- 2 cups leaf lettuce torn
- 3/4 cup cooked chicken cubed
- 2/3 cup fresh strawberries sliced
- 1 medium orange peeled and sectioned

- 1/4 cup strawberry syrup
- 2 tablespoons red wine vinegar
- 1/4 cup cashews

Direction

- Divide spinach and lettuce among 2 salad plates.
- Arrange chicken, strawberries and oranges on lettuce.
- Combine syrup and vinegar then drizzle over salads and top with cashews.

90. Strawberry Salad With Mandarin Oranges Recipe

Serving: 6 | Prep: | Cook: |Ready in:

Ingredients

- 6 cups torn mixed salad greens
- 1 cup fresh strawberries hulled and quartered
- 1/2 cup sliced green onions
- 1/2 cup canned rice noodles
- 1/4 cup sliced almonds toasted
- 11 ounce can mandarin orange slices drained
- 1/4 cup flaked coconut
- 2 teaspoons honey
- 2 teaspoons salad oil
- 2 teaspoons balsamic vinegar
- 1/2 teaspoon ground ginger
- 1/2 teaspoon salt
- 1/4 teaspoon pepper
- 2 ounces semi soft goat cheese crumbled

Direction

- In a large bowl combine greens, strawberries, onions, noodles and almonds then set aside.
- In blender combine 1/2 cup of the oranges, coconut, honey, oil, vinegar, ginger, salt, and pepper.
- Cover then process or blend until combined then pour dressing over salad and toss to coat.

- Top with remaining oranges and goat cheese then serve immediately.

91. Sweet Orange Amp Chicken Salad Recipe

Serving: 6 | Prep: | Cook: 10mins |Ready in:

Ingredients

- 1 bottle (8 oz.) CATALINA Fat Free Dressing , divided
- 4 boneless, skinless chicken breast halves (about 1-1/4 lb.)
- 1 red pepper , quartered
- 1 yellow pepper , quartered
- 1 green pepper , quartered
- 1 pkg. (10 oz.) salad greens
- 2 oranges , sectioned, pieces cut in half
- 1 Tbs toasted sesame seeds

Direction

- Brush 1/2 cup of the dressing on chicken and peppers.
- Grill or broil chicken and peppers 5 minutes on each side or until chicken is cooked through.
- Slice chicken diagonally into strips.
- Cut peppers into thin strips.
- Toss chicken, peppers, greens, oranges and remaining dressing. Sprinkle with sesame seeds.

92. Sweet Potato Orange Juice Salad Recipe

Serving: 6 | Prep: | Cook: 10mins |Ready in:

Ingredients

- 2 large sweet potatoes

- 1 cup marshmallows
- 1/2 cup orange juice
- 1/2 teaspoon grated orange rind
- 1 cup brown sugar
- 1 tablespoon flour
- 1/2 stick butter
- 1 teaspoon allspice
- 1/2 cup pecans

Direction

- Cook potatoes until tender then drain and cut into cubes then melt sugar and butter and add flour.
- Gradually add orange juice, rind and spice and mix thoroughly with sweet potatoes.
- Add pecans, raisins and marshmallows then chill and serve.

93. TANGY BEETY ORANGE SALAD Recipe

Serving: 4 | Prep: | Cook: |Ready in:

Ingredients

- Vinaigrette:
- 1/4 cup orange juice
- 1 tbsp orange zest
- 2 tbsp olive oil
- 1 tsp honey
- 1 tbsp balsamic vinegar
- salt and pepper to taste
- Salad:
- 2 cups cooked, sliced & cooled beets
- 1 small red onion, thinly sliced
- 1/2 cup crumbled feta
- 1 tbsp dillweed, chopped
- 1/3 cup chopped walnut pieces

Direction

- Combine all of the VINAIGRETTE ingredients and refrigerate.

- Meanwhile combine all of the SALAD ingredients with the exception of the walnuts.
- Toss dressing & salad just before serving.
- Top with walnuts.

94. Truly Sassy Sicilian Orange Salad Recipe

Serving: 4 | Prep: | Cook: |Ready in:

Ingredients

- 4 juicy oranges
- salt and freshly ground black pepper
- 10 black olives, pitted and cut in half
- 1 small white onion, thinly sliced
- 4 tbsp extra virgin olive oil

Direction

- Peel the oranges, taking care to remove all the white pith. Slice thinly and place in a salad bowl.
- Sprinkle with a little salt, then add the olives and onion.
- Drizzle with the oil and season with a generous grinding of pepper.

95. Warm Orange Spinach And Fennel Salad Recipe

Serving: 4 | Prep: | Cook: 5mins |Ready in:

Ingredients

- 1/2 cup orange juice with pulp
- 1 shallot, sliced
- 1 tbsp red wine vinegar
- 1 tsp Dijon mustard
- 1/4 tsp pepper
- 3 tbsp extra virgin olive oil
- 1 fennel (anise) bulb, finely sliced

- 4 blood oranges, peeling and sliced into rounds
- 4 cups baby spinach

Direction

- The salad dressing:
- In a small saucepan over medium high flame, combine orange juice, and 1/2 of the sliced shallot
- Bring to a boil and reduce volume to about 1/3 cup. This usually takes about 6 minutes
- Whisk in the vinegar, mustard, pepper, and 2 tbsp. olive oil
- In another skillet, over medium high flame, heat 1 tbsp. olive oil
- Add fennel and remaining shallot slices
- Sauté until tender crisp, about 1 minute
- To serve:
- Arrange blood orange slices on plates
- Top with baby spinach, shallots and fennel
- Drizzle with the warm dressing

96. Western Salad Recipe

Serving: 0 | Prep: | Cook: | Ready in:

Ingredients

- 1 cup mandarin oranges
- 1 cup pineapple chunks
- 1 cup shredded coconut
- 1 cup marshmallow bits
- 1 cup sour cream

Direction

- Mix ingredients together and chill. Serve as a salad with or without lettuce; or as a dessert.

Chapter 2: Pear Salad Recipes

***

97. Alouette Crumbled Blue Cheese Pear And Baby Arugula Salad Recipe

Serving: 4 | Prep: | Cook: 5mins | Ready in:

Ingredients

- 1 pkg.   Alouette® Crumbled blue cheese
- 1 ea.   Bartlette pear
- 12- 20   red grapes
- 1 bag   baby arugula salad
- 4 oz.   red wine vinaigrette

Direction

- * Remove arugula salad from bag and rinse and dry
- * Place in serving bowl
- * Split grapes in half and place on baby arugula
- * Split and remove core from the pear and slice into 1/8 inch slices and place on arugula
- * Pour red wine vinaigrette on salad and gently toss
- * Sprinkle Alouette® Crumbled Blue cheese on top and serve
- Alternative serving suggestions:
- Substitute the red wine vinaigrette for Champagne vinaigrette
- Add slivered walnuts for additional texture

98. Arugula, Pear & Gorgonzola Salad Recipe

Serving: 4 | Prep: | Cook: | Ready in:

Ingredients

- Vinaigrette:
- 3 oz extra virgin olive oil
- 1 oz white wine vinegar
- salt to taste
- Salad:
- 6 oz crumbled gorgonzola
- 6 cups arugula
- 1/2 cup toasted walnuts
- 1 ripe pear, cored, sliced thin

Direction

- Combine the olive oil & vinegar and whisk together. Salt to taste.
- In a salad bowl, toss the vinaigrette with the arugula, half of the walnuts & pear. Add the Gorgonzola and toss. Arrange on plate, top with remaining walnuts and pear slices.

99. Asian Pear Spinach And Golden Raisin Salad With Pomegranate Mustard Dressing And Herb Crusted Chicken Breast Recipe

Serving: 6 | Prep: | Cook: 15mins | Ready in:

Ingredients

- INGREDIENTS
- Pomegranate-Mustard Dressing
- 1/2 cup pomegranate juice
- 1 tablespoon honey
- 2 tablespoons Dijon mustard
- 1 tablespoon finely chopped shallot
- sea salt, to taste
- fresh ground black pepper, to taste
- 2 tablespoons canola oil
- 2 fresh ripe Asian pears, peeled and thinly sliced
- 4 cups (8 ounces) baby spinach leaves
- 3/4 cup California golden raisins
- herb Crusted chicken
- 6 boneless skinless chicken breasts (3 ounces each)
- sea salt, to taste
- fresh ground black pepper, to taste
- 1/2 cup chopped fresh Italian parsley
- 1/4 cup finely chopped fresh mint
- 1/4 cup chopped fresh chives
- 1/4 cup chopped fresh dill weed
- 1 tablespoon olive oil
- Toppings
- 1/2 cup fresh pomegranate seeds
- 1/2 cup finely slivered fresh mint
- Fresh chopped chives

Direction

- Pomegranate-Mustard Dressing
- Measure pomegranate juice into saucepan. Heat and simmer over medium-high heat until reduced to about 1/4 cup. Cool completely. Turn into blender. Add honey, mustard, shallot, salt and pepper. Pulse to mix well. With blender running, add oil in a slow steady stream. Set aside.
- Combine pears, spinach and raisins in a large mixing bowl. Add 1/4 cup dressing. Mix together and season to taste with salt and pepper. Cover and set aside to chill.
- Herb Crusted Chicken
- Season chicken breasts well on both sides with salt and pepper. Combine herbs in small bowl; mix well. Press liberal amount of herbs onto both sides of breasts. Heat oil in non-stick skillet over medium-high heat and sauté chicken about 4 minutes on both sides, until done (170°F).
- To Serve
- Arrange salad on large individual serving plates. Thinly slice chicken breasts and arrange on top. Drizzle with dressing and top with pomegranate seeds, mint and chives.

100. Asian Pear And Watercress Salad With Sesame Dressing Recipe

Serving: 4 | Prep: | Cook: | Ready in:

Ingredients

- 1/2" thick slice peeled fresh ginger
- 1/4 cup Asian sesame paste
- 3 tablespoons Asian sesame oil
- 1/4 cup rice vinegar
- 1-1/2 tablespoons sugar
- 2 tablespoons water
- 1 teaspoon Asian chili paste with garlic
- 1/2 teaspoon salt
- Salad:
- 2 medium Asian pears
- 4 cups trimmed watercress sprigs
- 1 carrot finely shredded

Direction

- Blend all dressing ingredients in a blender until smooth.
- Peel pear and cut into julienne strips then transfer to a bowl.
- Combine watercress and pear in a bowl then season with salt and pepper and toss gently.
- Divide among plates then drizzle with some dressing and sprinkle with carrot.

101. Autumn Harvest Salad Recipe Recipe

Serving: 0 | Prep: | Cook: 30mins | Ready in:

Ingredients

- Salad
- • ½ lb. baby spinach
- • 2 pears, sliced
- • ~2 tsp. lemon juice
- • blue cheese crumbles
- • pecans
- • dried cranberries
- Dressing
- • 1/4 cup balsamic vinegar
- • ½ tsp. salt
- • ½ tsp. ground pepper
- • 1 Tbs. raspberry jam (optional)
- • 2/3 c. extra virgin olive oil

Direction

- 1 Make the dressing: Whisk together the vinegar, salt, pepper and jam (if using). Slowly add the olive oil and whisk until emulsified. Let stand for at least 30 minutes, or up to 3 hours.
- 2 Prep the pears: As you slice the pears, put them in a bowl with the lemon juice to keep them from turning brown.
- 3 Assemble the salad: Just before serving, place the spinach into a bowl and mix with enough dressing to lightly coat the leaves. Put the dressed spinach on a serving platter. Top the greens with the pear slices (drained of any lemon juice), blue cheese, pecans, and dried cranberries. Pour a little extra dressing over the top.
- (If you have time, and want to kick this salad up another notch, you can prepare and use candied pecans.)

102. Barbecued Pear Beet And Leek Salad With Blue Cheese Dressing Recipe

Serving: 4 | Prep: | Cook: 60mins | Ready in:

Ingredients

- 2 beets, blanched briefly in boiling water, peeled and cut into 1/2" sticks
- 2 pears, just ripe, sliced into quarters lengthwise through the stem ends, core removed

- 2 leeks cleaned and trimmed.
- 2 tbsp olive oil
- 1 bottle or can of beer
- 1 cup balsamic vinegar
- 1/2 cup blue cheese, crumbled

Direction

- Preheat grill to medium heat (about 350°F).
- Wrap beet sticks in foil and roast on grill about 45 – 60 minutes or until tender. Set pouch aside.
- While beets are cooking combine the beer and balsamic vinegar in a saucepan and bring to a gentle boil. Continue to simmer until liquid has reduced by about half and become syrupy. Set aside.
- Liberally oil the grill with the 2 tbsp. of olive oil. Place leeks on the grill for 3 – 4 minutes turning several times. Add the pears to the grill and continue grilling leeks and pears for 3 – 4 minutes, turning both several times, until tender and lightly charred. Slice the leeks into 1 inch chunks and place with beet sticks and pear pieces in a serving bowl.
- Pour the reduced beer and balsamic dressing over and toss. Garnish with the crumbled blue cheese and serve immediately.

103. Blue Cheese And Pear Salad Recipe

Serving: 4 | Prep: | Cook: | Ready in:

Ingredients

- 1 bunch arugula torn
- 1 head romaine lettuce torn
- 3 medium fresh cored and thinly sliced pears
- 1/2 cup buttermilk
- 1/2 cup blue cheese
- 1 medium garlic cloves minced
- 1/4 teaspoon freshly ground black pepper
- 3 tablespoons chopped toasted walnuts

Direction

- Divide arugula and romaine among plates then arrange pears on greens.
- Combine buttermilk, cheese, garlic and pepper.
- Toss and pour over lettuce and sprinkle with walnuts and serve.

104. Blue Cheese And Pear Salad With Candied Pecans Recipe

Serving: 8 | Prep: | Cook: 5mins | Ready in:

Ingredients

- candied Pecans:
- ¼ cup white sugar
- ½ cup pecans, coarsely chopped
- Dressing:
- ⅓ cup olive oil
- 3 tablespoons white wine vinegar
- 1 tablelspoon white sugar
- a good shot of honey (I'd guess I squirt in about a heaping tablespoon)
- 1½ teaspoons prepared mustard
- 1 clove garlic, minced
- ½ teaspoon salt
- 2 or 3 twists of fresh ground black pepper
- Salad ingredients:
- ½ head iceberg lettuce, chopped into bite-size pieces (or you can use romaine)
- ½ bag of spinach, chopped into bite-size pieces
- 2 pears, peeled and cored and chopped, and sprinkled with fruit Fresh to prevent browning
- 6 ounces Roquefort or blue cheese, crumbled (I prefer to use a block of blue cheese so I can make bigger chunks than what you usually get in the pre-crumbled cheese tubs)
- ½ cup chopped sweet onion

Direction

- Prepare the pecans first, so they can cool off.

47

- In a skillet over medium heat, stir ¼ cup of sugar together with the pecans (watch carefully, as these will burn easily - you want a hot flame, but not so hot that it will scorch the sugar).
- Continue stirring constantly until sugar has melted completely and the pecans are beginning to turn a beautiful caramel color.
- Carefully (I say "carefully" because this is some HOT stuff - don't burn yourself) transfer nuts onto a cutting board to cool completely, separating the nuts as they cool (otherwise they will cool in a big "clump" and you will need to break it all up, making for some "not so pretty" candied pecans!).
- NOTE - VERY IMPORTANT! Do not put the nuts on waxed paper to cool - I did that the first time I made this, not realizing that the nuts would stick to the waxed paper...I couldn't remove them to save my soul - I had to throw out the entire batch and start all over!! I've found that my cutting board works best - you can scrape up any "stuck" nuts with a spatula, and it's easy to clean up.
- For the dressing, blend oil and vinegar together with a whisk, then add remaining dressing ingredients, whisking until it is well blended (it will tend to separate as it sits, so just give it a good stir before dressing the salad with it).
- Set dressing aside until ready to serve the salad.
- When ready to serve, toss lettuce, spinach, pears, blue cheese, and onions in a large bowl.
- Pour dressing over salad, sprinkle with pecans; toss and serve immediately.
- Unfortunately, this salad does not keep well once it is "dressed". Scale it down (or increase amounts) to make only what you think you will eat at one time. The dressing will keep well in the refrigerator for some time, so extra dressing is not a problem - it will be ready and waiting next time you're craving this salad.

105.   Blue Cheese Pear And Pecan Salad With Warm Bacon Dressing Recipe

Serving: 10 | Prep: | Cook: 10mins | Ready in:

Ingredients

- Toast:
- 1   cup pecan halves or pieces
- Combine; Toss with pecans and Roast:
- 2   T. sugar
- 1   T. vegetable oil
- 1/2   t. kosher salt
- 1/2   t. ground cinnamon
- 1/4   t. ground ginger
- 1/4   t. dry mustard
- 1/8   t. ground nutmeg
- 1/8   t. ground cloves
- Pinch cayenne
- For the Warm bacon Dressing—
- Saute:
- 6   slices (8 oz.) thick-sliced bacon, diced
- Add and Saute:
- 1/4   cup shallots, minced (about 3 shallots)
- Stir in:
- 1   T. honey mustard
- 1   t. ground cinnamon
- Whisk in:
- 1/2   cup apple juice concentrate
- 1/4   cup extra-virgin olive oil
- 1   T. apple cider vinegar
- salt and pepper to taste
- For the Salad—
- Toss Together:
- 12   cups mesclun salad greens
- 1   cup fennel bulb, thinly sliced
- 1   firm yet ripe bosc pear, cored and thinly sliced
- 1/2   cup Maytag, Roquefort, or other good-quality blue cheese, crumbled
- Prepared pecans and dressing

Direction

- Preheat oven to 350°.

48

- Toast pecans on a baking sheet in oven until golden, about 10 minutes.
- Combine sugar, oil, salt, and spices in a small bowl while nuts toast. Toss hot pecans with sugar mixture until well coated. Return nuts to baking sheet and roast 8–10 more minutes, or until coating is dry. Do not over bake.
- Sauté bacon for the dressing in a medium skillet over medium-high heat until crisp. Spoon off excess fat; leave bacon in skillet.
- Add the shallots to the skillet; sauté until softened, about 3 minutes.
- Stir in the mustard and cinnamon; cook another minute.
- Whisk in the apple juice concentrate, oil, and vinegar. Season with salt and pepper. Keep dressing warm over low heat until ready to toss the salad.
- Toss the greens, fennel, pear, blue cheese, and spiced pecans with some of the warm dressing (you may not use all the dressing). Serve salad immediately.

- Quarter the unpeeled pears lengthwise, remove and discard the cores and then, using a sharp knife, a mandoline or a vegetable peeler, carve each quarter into slices between 1/8- and 1/4-inch thick.
- Layer the fennel and pear loosely on a platter or individual plates. Using a vegetable peeler or cheese slicer, shave the cheese into curls or ribbons and intersperse them with the pear and cheese.
- If desired, toast the walnuts in a dry skillet over medium heat, shaking the skillet occasionally, just until they are warmed, about 3 minutes.
- Scatter the walnuts over the salad. Drizzle each salad with 1 to 2 tablespoons of oil, being careful to cover as much of the ingredients as possible. Then sprinkle drops of vinegar over each salad, using a scant 1 tablespoon for each plate. The oil should form a slick surface over the salad, and the vinegar should form tiny chestnut-colored drops atop the oil.

106. Bosc Pear And Fennel Salad Recipe

Serving: 4 | Prep: | Cook: |Ready in:

Ingredients

- 2 medium (about 1 pound) fennel bulbs
- 2 ripe Bosc or Asian pears
- 4 ounces pecorino or parmigiano-Reggiano (Parmesan) cheese
- 4 ounces (about 1 cup) walnut halves
- 1 cup extra-virgin olive oil
- 1/3 cup balsamic vinegar, preferably aged

Direction

- Trim the stems from the fennel, cut out the cores and remove the tough outer layers. Slice the fennel lengthwise into thin, sickle-shaped slices.

107. Breaded Barlett Pear Salad Recipe

Serving: 4 | Prep: | Cook: 5mins |Ready in:

Ingredients

- 1/3 cup extra virgin olive oil
- 1/4 cup freshly squeezed lemon juice
- 2 teaspoons chopped fresh parsley
- 1 clove garlic minced
- 1/4 teaspoon kosher salt
- 1/2 teaspoon freshly ground black pepper
- Salad:
- 1/2 cup all purpose flour
- 1/4 teaspoon salt
- 1/4 teaspoon ground white pepper
- 1/4 teaspoon paprika
- 3/4 cup seasoned dry bread crumbs
- 1/4 cup extra virgin olive oil
- 4 eggs lightly beaten

- 4 ripe bartlett pears cored and quartered
- 4 cups vegetable oil for frying
- 6 ounces prosciutto sliced very thin
- 4 cups mixed baby field greens
- 2 teaspoons aged balsamic vinegar

Direction

- In large mixing bowl combine olive oil, lemon juice, parsley, garlic, kosher salt and pepper.
- Whisk until well blended then cover and refrigerate several hours to meld flavors.
- In small shallow bowl combine flour, salt, white pepper and paprika then set aside.
- In another shallow bowl toss bread crumbs with olive oil then set aside.
- Dredge pear quarters in seasoned flour then dip in beaten egg then drain off excess.
- Roll in crumb mixture then preheat oil in deep fryer to 350.
- Fry pears 2 pieces at a time until golden then drain on paper towels
- Whisk vinaigrette again and toss greens with half the dressing.
- Arrange prosciutto on 4 salad plates then mound greens in center of plates.
- Warm with warm pear quarters then drizzle remaining vinaigrette over salads.
- Sprinkle with pepper then drizzle balsamic over top.

108.   California Walnut Pear Bistro Salad Recipe

Serving: 4 | Prep: | Cook: |Ready in:

Ingredients

- 8 cups assorted torn salad greens
- 2 fresh bartlett pears, cored and sliced
- 1/2 cup California walnut pieces
- 1/4 cup dried cranberries (optional)
- 1/2 cup crumbled blue cheese
- 1/3 cup balsamic or raspberry vinaigrette

Direction

- Line large salad platter with greens; top with pear, walnuts and dried cranberries.
- Sprinkle with cheese.
- Drizzle dressing over salad.
- Serve with crusty bread, if desired.

109.   Crab Salad With Hazelnuts And Pear Recipe

Serving: 4 | Prep: | Cook: |Ready in:

Ingredients

- 1 1/2 cups fresh lump crab meat
- 1/4 cup chopped roasted hazelnuts
- 1/2 cup finely chopped celery
- 2 firm, but sweet pears, finely chopped
- 1/4 cup finely chopped red onion
- 2 Tbsp finely chopped fresh parsley
- 2 Tbsp lemon juice
- 1 Tbsp olive oil
- Freshly ground pepper
- salt and pepper to taste
- 4 large pieces of butter lettuce, rinsed and patted dry

Direction

- In a medium sized bowl mix the hazelnuts, celery, pear, onion, parsley, lemon juice, olive oil, ground pepper, and salt.
- Gently fold in the lump crab meat, trying not to break up the crab too much.
- Make individual servings, about a half cup each over a piece of butter lettuce.

110.   Creamy Balsamic Pear Salad Recipe

Serving: 6 | Prep: | Cook: 15mins |Ready in:

Ingredients

- 1/4 c balsamic vinaigrette Dressing
- 2 TB mayonnaise
- 6 c torn mixed salad greens
- 2 red pears,thinly sliced
- 1/2 c shredded Italian Three cheese Blend
- 1/3 c slivered red onions
- 4 slices bacon,cooked,crumbled

Direction

- Add dressing gradually to mayonnaise, stirring with a fork or whisk until well blended
- Combine remaining ingredients in large bowl.
- Add dressing mixture; toss to coat. Serve immediately.

---

111. Curried Cashew Pear And Grape Salad Recipe

Serving: 6 | Prep: | Cook: 15mins | Ready in:

Ingredients

- 3/4 cup cashew halves
- 4 slices bacon, coarsely chopped
- 1 tablespoon melted butter
- 1 teaspoon chopped fresh rosemary
- 1 teaspoon curry powder
- 1 tablespoon brown sugar
- 1/2 teaspoon kosher salt
- 1/2 teaspoon cayenne pepper
- Dressing:
- 3 tablespoons white wine vinegar
- 3 tablespoons Dijon mustard
- 2 tablespoons honey
- 1/2 cup olive oil
- salt and black pepper to taste
- Salad:
- 1 (10 ounce) package mixed salad greens
- 1/2 medium bosc pear, thinly sliced
- 1/2 cup halved seedless red grapes

Direction

- In a large, dry skillet over medium-high heat, toast cashews until golden brown, about 5 minutes.
- Remove cashews to a dish to cool slightly.
- Return skillet to medium-high heat, cook bacon strips until crisp on both sides, about 7 minutes.
- Remove bacon with a slotted spoon, and soak up grease with a paper towel.
- Coarsely chop bacon, and set aside.
- In a medium bowl, stir together butter, rosemary, curry powder, brown sugar, salt, cayenne pepper, and toasted cashews. Set aside.
- In a small bowl, stir together white wine vinegar, mustard, and honey.
- Slowly whisk in olive oil, and sprinkle with salt and pepper to taste.
- In a large salad bowl, toss dressing with greens, pear slices, grapes, and bacon, and sprinkle with nut mixture.

---

112. Elegant Crab Salad With Pear And Hazelnuts Recipe

Serving: 4 | Prep: | Cook: | Ready in:

Ingredients

- 1 1/2 cups fresh lump crab meat
- 1/4 cup chopped roasted hazelnuts
- 1/2 cup finely chopped celery
- 2 firm, but sweet pears, finely chopped
- 1/4 cup finely chopped red onion
- 2 Tbsp finely chopped fresh parsley
- 2 Tbsp lemon juice (or 3 Tbsp Meyer lemon juice)
- 1 Tbsp olive oil
- Freshly ground pepper
- salt and pepper to taste
- 4 large pieces of butter lettuce, rinsed and patted dry

Direction

- In a medium sized bowl mix the hazelnuts, celery, pear, onion, parsley, lemon juice, olive oil, ground pepper, and salt.
- Gently fold in the lump crab meat, trying not to break up the crab too much.
- Make individual servings, about a half cup each over a piece of butter lettuce.

---

113. Festive Cranberry Pear Salad Recipe

Serving: 8 | Prep: | Cook: 12mins | Ready in:

Ingredients

- 1/2 c. cider vinegar
- 1/4 c. cranberries
- 1/4 c. olive oil
- 2 t. sugar
- 1/8 t. salt
- 1/8 t. pepper
- 2 red pears, cored
- 2 heads romaine lettuce, torn into bite-size pieces
- 2 heads Belgian endive, chopped
- 1/2 c. plus 2 T. chopped walnuts, toasted and divided
- 1/2 c. crumbled gorgonzola cheese

Direction

- Toast the walnuts just until you smell them.
- Combine vinegar and cranberries in a saucepan over medium heat; cook until cranberries are tender.
- Remove from heat; add oil, sugar, salt and pepper.
- Place in a blender and process until smooth; chill.
- Thinly slice one pear; dice remaining pear.
- In a large bowl, toss together greens, diced pear, 1/2 cup walnuts and cheese.
- Drizzle with dressing and toss to coat.

- Divide among 8 salad plates; top with sliced pear and remaining nuts.

---

114. Freah Pear And Cherry Salad With Vanilla Pear Vinaigrette Recipe

Serving: 2 | Prep: | Cook: 5mins | Ready in:

Ingredients

- 1/4 cup white sugar
- 1 tps. ground cinnamon
- 3 Tbs. white wine vinegar
- 3 Tbs. far-free vanilla yogurt
- 2 Tbs. honey
- 3/4 tps. kosher salt
- 1 (15.25 oz.) can pears in light syrup, drained reserving syrup
- 1/4 tps. freshly ground black pepper
- 1 tps. vanilla extract
- 1 pinch ground nutmeg
- 1/2 (10oz.) package minex salad greens
- 1/2 (10 oz.) bag spinach leaves
- 1 pear-pelled, cored and sliced
- 1/2 cup dried cherries
- 1/3 cup crumbled feta cheese
- 1 cup walnuts

Direction

- 1. Combine sugar, cinnamon, and walnuts in a skillet over medium heat. Mix together until sugar and cinnamon are melted and walnuts are evenly coated. Remove from heat. Spread walnuts on a large plate to cool
- 2. In the container of a blender, combine the drained pears, 1/3 cup of the reserved syrup from the can, vinegar, yogurt, honey, salt, pepper, vanilla extract, and nutmeg; blend until smooth.
- 3. Assemble the salad by tossing together the mixed greens, spinach, pear slices, dried

cherries, feta cheese, and walnuts in a serving bowl. Serve with dressing on the side.

115. Fresh Fruit & Spinach Salad Recipe

Serving: 1 | Prep: | Cook: 5mins | Ready in:

Ingredients

- 2 large handfuls fresh baby spinach
- 1/2 ripe d'anjou pear, diced
- 6 large strawberries, hulled & stems removed, then diced
- 1 large handful fresh blueberries
- about 1/4 cup crumbled feta cheese
- 6 or 7 almonds, finely chopped
- for the dressing
- 3 Tbsp balsamic vinegar
- 1 Tbsp pure honey
- 1 dash of each: kosher salt, ground black pepper, dried oregano

Direction

- Whisk dressing ingredients together in a small bowl.
- Add in your spinach and toppings, toss, & enjoy! :)

116. Fresh Pear And Gorgonzola Salad Recipe

Serving: 4 | Prep: | Cook: 5mins | Ready in:

Ingredients

- 1 Cup walnut halves/Pieces
- 4 - 6 Cups Torn mixed greens
- 1/2 Cup vinaigrette (I use La Martinique. . .it's the best with this recipe)
- 2 pears, peeled, cored & sliced

- 1/4 C gorgonzola (or to taste)

Direction

- Place walnuts in dry skillet and turn the heat to medium.
- Toast, shaking the pan frequently, until they are aromatic and begin to darken in color; 3 - 5 minutes.
- Set aside and let cool.
- Toss the greens and most of the vinaigrette.
- Divide among 4 plates.
- Cover with pear slices.
- Sprinkle crumbled Gorgonzola all over.
- Crumble or chop walnuts, then scatter over the salad.
- Drizzle remaining vinaigrette over salad and serve.
- Enjoy.

117. Gorgonzola Pear Salad Recipe

Serving: 4 | Prep: | Cook: | Ready in:

Ingredients

- 6 cups mixed greens trimmed washed and dried
- 1/2 cup vinaigrette
- 2 pears cored and sliced
- 1/4 pound gorgonzola cheese crumbled
- 1 cup walnut halves toasted and coarsely chopped
- Vinaigrette:
- 1 tablespoon finely chopped red onion
- 1 teaspoon Dijon style mustard
- 1/4 cup red wine vinegar
- 1 teaspoon salt
- 1 teaspoon freshly ground black pepper
- 3/4 cup extra virgin olive oil

Direction

- Toss greens with a half cup of the vinaigrette and divide between individual salad plates.
- Arrange pear slices on top and sprinkle cheese all over.
- Top with walnuts and remaining vinaigrette.
- To make vinaigrette combine onion, mustard, vinegar, salt and pepper in a small mixing bowl and whisk until thoroughly combined.
- Add the oil in a thin stream whisking constantly.

118. Grape And Pear Salad With Honey Dressing Recipe

Serving: 4 | Prep: | Cook: | Ready in:

Ingredients

- 3 cups washed, fresh spinach leaves
- 1 cup red grapes- seedless
- 1 large pear,sliced
- 3/4 cup sliced celery
- 3/4 cup chopped pecans
- 1/2 cup lemon juice (fresh squeezed best)
- 4 tablespoons oil
- 4 tablespoons honey

Direction

- Blend 1/2 cup lemon juice, oil and honey together and refrigerate awhile to blend flavors.
- Place the spinach leaves on a large plate and top with the grapes, pecans, celery and pear slices
- Drizzle with a bit of the refrigerated dressing. Add more dressing when serving if desired.

119. Grilled Pear And Watercress Salad Recipe

Serving: 6 | Prep: | Cook: 15mins | Ready in:

Ingredients

- 2 Tablespoons firmly packed brown sugar
- 1 Tablespoon water
- 1/4 teaspoon freshly ground pepper
- 2 Tablespoons chopped walnuts
- 2 firm yet ripe pears, cored and cut into 6 lengthwise wedges, peel intact
- lemon juice for brushing
- Vinaigrette Dressing:
- 2 Tablespoons fresh lemon juice, plus extra for brushing
- 1 Tablespoon rice vinegar
- 1 teaspoon Dijon mustard
- 1 Tablespoon minced shallot
- 1/4 teaspoon salt
- 1/4 teaspoon freshly ground pepper
- 1 Tablespoon extra-virgin olive oil
- 6 cups watercress sprigs, tough stems removed
- 3 Tablespoons crumbled blue cheese

Direction

- Prepare a hot fire in a charcoal grill or preheat a gas grill or broiler.
- Away from the heat source, lightly coat the grill rack or broiler pan with cooking spray. Position the cooking rack 4-6 inches from the heat source.
- In a small frying pan over medium heat, combine the brown sugar, water, and pepper. Cook, stirring constantly, until the sugar dissolves.
- Stir in the walnuts, reduce the heat to low, and cook for 30 seconds. Remove from the heat and quickly spread the nuts on a sheet of parchment (baking) paper or a plate. Set aside and let cool.
- Brush the pear wedges with lemon juice and arrange on the grill or broiler pan. Grill or broil turning once, until the pears begin to brown, 3-4 minutes total. Set aside.
- To make the vinaigrette in a small bowl, whisk together the 2 Tablespoons lemon juice, the rice vinegar, the mustard, and the shallot. Add the salt and pepper and whisk to blend. While

whisking, slowly add the olive oil in a thin stream until emulsified.

- In a large bowl, combine the watercress and blue cheese. Pour the vinaigrette over the salad and toss gently to mix well and coat evenly.
- To serve, divide the salad among individual plates.
- Place 2 pear wedges on each, then sprinkle with the walnuts

120.   Grilled Pear Salad Recipe

Serving: 4 | Prep: | Cook: 6mins |Ready in:

Ingredients

- mixed salad greens
- THINLY SLICED cucumbER
- roastED pecans
- ½ pear PER PERSON CUT IN HALF, PEELED, SLICED AND FANNED AND PAINTED WITH butter. GRILLED TILL GOLDEN.
- blue cheese.
- VINAGRETTE DRESSING: oil,wine vinegar, mustard powder, sugar, salt & pepper.

Direction

- PLACE LETTUCE LEAVES ON EACH PLATE. SPREAD WITH CUCUMBERS. ONCE PEARS ARE GRILLED PLACE A CUBE OF BLUE CHEESE ONTOP AND GRILL TILL MELTED. PLACE ONTOP OF SALAD WHILE STILL WARM. DRESS AND SPRINKLE ROASTED PEACANS AND SERVE WARM.

121.   Lime Pear Salad Recipe

Serving: 8 | Prep: | Cook: |Ready in:

Ingredients

- 16 ounce carton cottage cheese
- 8 ounce container frozen whipped topping thawed
- 3 ounce package lime gelatin
- 20 ounce can sliced pears drained
- 1/2 cup shredded coconut
- 1 cup chopped toasted pecans

Direction

- Combine cottage cheese and whipped topping in a large mixing bowl.
- Sprinkle dry gelatin over top and stir to mix.
- Fold in drained fruit.
- Stir in pecans just before serving.

122.   Mamas Pear Salad Recipe

Serving: 6 | Prep: | Cook: |Ready in:

Ingredients

- 1 can pear halves
- mayonnaise
- cheddar cheese, grated
- lettuce or spinach leaves

Direction

- Chill pears in can
- Open can and drain pears
- Place one or two pear halves on leaf of lettuce or bed of spinach leaves
- Place about 1 tsp of mayonnaise on pear half and top with shredded cheddar cheese.

123.   Mesclun Arugula Fennel Salad With Prosciutto And Pear Vinaigrette Recipe

Serving: 4 | Prep: | Cook: |Ready in:

Ingredients

- 2/3 cup pear nectar
- 1/4 cup seasoned rice vinegar
- 1/4 teaspoon salt
- 1 teaspoon freshly ground black pepper
- 1 fennel bulb
- 5 ounces mesclun salad greens
- 1 cup arugula leaves torn into pieces
- 2 ounces thinly sliced prosciutto julienned
- 4 ripe figs quartered through the stem end
- 1 ounce parmigiano Reggiano cheese

Direction

- In a small bowl stir together the pear nectar and vinegar.
- Season with salt and pepper and set aside.
- Cut off the stems and feathery tops and any bruised outer stalks from the fennel bulb.
- Cut the fennel bulb in half lengthwise and cut away and discard the core.
- Slice crosswise paper thin then set aside.
- In a bowl combine the mesclun and arugula.
- Add half of the dressing and toss well.
- Divide greens evenly among individual plates.
- Top greens with the fennel, prosciutto and figs and drizzle with the remaining dressing.
- Using a vegetable peeler shave thin slices from the cheese and sprinkle over the salads.
- Season with pepper and serve.

---

124.   Mixed Green Salad With Bacon Wrapped Pears Recipe

Serving: 4 | Prep: | Cook: 30mins | Ready in:

Ingredients

- 1 pear of your choice (I used a green anjou)
- 1/2 pound thick sliced pepper bacon, sliced in half and also cut lengthwise in half
- whipped honey (see #3 in directions)
- 1 cup washed baby arugula
- 1/2 cup washed spinach
- 1/4 washed and chopped romaine
- A healthy chunk of creamy gorgonzola (I rarely measure cheese, especially in salads, adjust to your own preferences and taste)
- 10-15 cherry tomatoes, sliced in half
- 4 TBLS slivered almonds
- Reduced Balsamic to taste, used as dressing to drizzle (recipe below)
- 2 TBLS basil infused olive oil (I simply purchased this at the store)
- Reduced Balsamic
- 1/2 cup aged balsamic
- pinch of sugar (this is not necessary if your balsamic has been thoroughly aged, about 10 years or more)

Direction

- (Preheat oven to 375 degrees)
- Wash pear thoroughly, cut into thick slices (I had about 12-14 thick slices of pear)
- Wrap slices of bacon around each slice of pear, secure with a toothpick and place on a wire rack above a sided cookie sheet prepared with aluminum foil (for easy clean-up).
- Place a small dollop of whipped honey on top of each pear/bacon combo. (This will create a sugary caramelized crust on top of the peppery bacon).
- Place bacon wrapped pears in the oven for approx. 15 minutes, after 15 minutes flip the bacon wrapped pears over and continue to roast for another 10-15 minutes until bacon is cooked, juicy and crisp.
- While the pears are cooking: place arugula, spinach, romaine, gorgonzola, almonds, tomatoes in a large bowl and toss.
- When the pears are finished roasting allow them to cool for about 5 minutes.
- Place slightly cooled pears atop your salad mixture.
- Drizzle with reduced balsamic and basil infused olive oil and toss.
- Reduced Balsamic
- Place balsamic (and sugar if using it) in a saucepan over medium heat.
- Whisking constantly bring to a simmer.

- Continue to whisk and simmer for about 15 minutes, until balsamic is thick and syrupy.
- Cool.
- Eat it and enjoy!

---

125. Mixed Greens And Pear Salad Recipe

Serving: 8 | Prep: | Cook: 10mins | Ready in:

Ingredients

- 1/3 cup pecan halves
- 1/2 tsp. cinnamon sugar
- 5 cups torn mixed salad greens
- 1 large pear, thinly sliced
- 1/2 cup colby & monterey jack cheese Crumbles
- 1/4 cup dried cranberries
- 1/3 cup Zesty Italian dressing

Direction

- PLACE pecans in microwaveable pie plate sprayed with cooking spray. Sprinkle with cinnamon sugar; toss to coat. Spread evenly onto bottom of pie plate. Microwave on HIGH 1 to 1-1/2 min. or until toasted, stirring every 30 sec.
- MEANWHILE, toss greens with pears, cheese and cranberries in large bowl.
- ADD pecans and dressing just before serving; mix lightly.

---

126. Mushroom Stuffed Pork Tenderloin And Mache Salad With Pear Gorgonzola And Honey Walnuts Recipe

Serving: 6 | Prep: | Cook: 45mins | Ready in:

Ingredients

- For the Pork Tenderloin:
- 1 pork tenderloin, weighing about 1 pound
- 2 Tbsp butter, softened
- sea salt and fresh black pepper
- ~~~~~~~~~~~~~~~~~~~~~~~~~~~~~~~~ ~~~~~~~~~~~~~~~~~~
- For the stuffing:
- 2 tbsp butter, divided
- 1 medium onion, finely chopped
- 3 sprigs of thyme, leaves only
- 4 fresh sage leaves, minced
- 1/2 cup mushrooms, finely chopped
- 1/2 cup fresh breadcrumbs (use a good loaf of bread, cut off crusts, pulse a few times in a food processor)
- 4 tbsp chopped fresh parsley
- grated zest of 1 lemon
- 2 tsp. lemon juice
- 1 egg beaten with 2 tbsp cream (if you do not like eggs/have eggs, you could omit the egg and just use a 3 tbsp heavy cream. Your stuffing will just be a bit crumblier)
- ~~~~~~~~~~~~~~~~~~~~~~~~~~~~~~~~ ~~~~~~~~~~~~~~~~~~
- For the salad:
- 1 bag Mâche (lambs lettuce)
- 2 ripe small pears, diced
- 1 cup walnuts, toasted then glazed with honey while warm
- 1 cup gorgonzola cheese, crumbled (room temp to serve)
- ~~~~~~~~~~~~~~~~~~~~~~~~~~~~~~~~ ~~~~~~~~~~~~~~~~~~
- Balsamic honey Vinaigrette:
- 1/4 cup aged balsamic vinegar
- 1 tablespoon honey
- 1/2 cup olive oil
- pinch of sea salt

Direction

- Balsamic Honey Vinaigrette: Place all ingredients in a small jar and shake well. Set aside.
- Preheat oven to 350 F
- Slit the tenderloin(s) in half lengthwise and then using a rolling pin or a flat (not toothed)

meat mallet to pound the two halves flatter and to make them a bit wider. Season the pork with salt and pepper.

- Make the Stuffing:
- Melt the butter in a frying pan and sauté the onions gently until soft. Add the herbs and stir once or twice. Add the mushrooms and raise the heat just a bit. Add a pinch of salt and stir. The mushroom should exude some juice. When the juices have almost evaporated, empty the contents of the pan into a bowl. Allow it to cool slightly and add the rest of the ingredients. Stir the mixture together and season with salt and pepper.
- Spoon the stuffing on to one half of the tenderloin. Pat it down lightly to keep it a bit firm. Place the other half on top. Smear with 1 tbsp. of the softened butter. Using kitchen twine tie everything together at about inch and a half to two inch intervals to make a nice bundle.
- Using the other tbsp. softened butter, grease the bottom of a roasting pan.
- Carefully transfer the tenderloin to the pan and bake in the oven for about 45 minutes (check after 30 with a meat thermometer). When the roast is cooked, remove it from the pan to a cutting board. Tent with foil.
- In a salad bowl, gently toss the Mâche and pears with a light drizzle of the vinaigrette. Keep chilled while carving the roast.
- Remove the strings from the roast and carve across into tenderloin.
- Distribute salad to serving plates and sprinkle with walnuts and gorgonzola. Fan the pork alongside. Drizzle any remaining vinaigrette around plate, if desired.

---

127. Pear Rocket And Blue Cheese Salad Recipe

Serving: 4 | Prep: | Cook: 30mins | Ready in:

Ingredients

- 2 PEARS FRESH PEARS
- 2 BUNCH ROCKET ITALIAN MIX SALAD
- 100G BLUE CHEESES
- 80G WALNUTS
- 2 TBSP VEG OIL
- 2 TBSP ICEING SUGAR
- SALT & PEPPER
- FOR VINAGIRGRETTE
- 150ML OLIVE OIL
- 50ML BALSAMIC VINGER
- 1 TBSP HONEY

Direction

- Peel Pears with peeler cut them into slices
- Caramelize the pears heat frying pan over high heat add 2 tbsp. veg oil then carefully spoon in pear wedges make sure they all have contact with bottom of pan while caramelizing turn the pears as they tend to burn you also want to brown all over season the pears with salt and pepper when golden brown remove pears from pan place onto a tray to cool
- Caramelize walnuts add walnuts to hot pan and caramelize for 2 mins add icing sugar mix well turn off heat mix well then place on try salt and pepper
- Make vinaigrette
- Then add the salad walnuts blue cheese pears then add vinaigrette

---

128. Pear And Blue Cheese Salad Recipe

Serving: 4 | Prep: | Cook: | Ready in:

Ingredients

- 4 Ripe pears
- 4 oz blue cheese (Maytag!!)
- 2 tsp balsamic vinegar
- 4 tsp olive oil
- salt and pepper
- arugula salad mix
- walnuts (Optional)

Direction

- Cut the pears into quarters and remove the cores.
- Clean the Argula Salad Mix.
- Using a large serving platter, arrange the salad mix.
- Thinly slice each pear quarter and arrange on the salad mix.
- Cut the cheese into bitesize pieces or crumble roughly, and scatter over the pear and salad mix.
- Wisk the oil and vinegar together and drizzle over the salad.
- Season with salt and pepper and serve! Garnish with walnut slices.
- Easy and elegant!

129. Pear And Pecan Salad Recipe

Serving: 4 | Prep: | Cook: 15mins | Ready in:

Ingredients

- 6 cups mixed torn salad greens
- 3 oz. fresh goat cheese (or as much as you enjoy) :)
- 2 tbsp. red wine vinegar
- 6 tbsp. olive oil
- 1 tsp. Dijon mustard
- 1/4 tsp. salt
- fresh ground pepper to taste
- 1 1/2 ripe pears
- 3 tbsp. unsalted butter (I just use margarine)
- 1 1/2 tbsp. granulated sugar
- 1/2 cup pecan halves (or to suit)

Direction

- Wash and pat lettuce dry with paper towels and put in a salad bowl.
- With your fingers, coarsely crumble the goat cheese and sprinkle the crumbles over the greens. Cover the salad bowl with plastic wrap and refrigerate until ready to serve.
- Just before serving, make the dressing. Put the vinegar, olive oil, mustard, salt and pepper in a small bowl. Whisk until the ingredients are blended. Set the dressing aside.
- Peel each pear and with a small, sharp knife, quarter each pear lengthwise. Cut away the stem and core from the pear quarters. Cut each pear quarter lengthwise in half so you end up with about 24 wedges.
- Put the butter in a large nonstick frying pan. Set the pan on medium and melt the butter. Add the pear wedges and sauté for 1 minute, gently turning the pears with the spatula to coat the pears with butter. Sprinkle the sugar over the pears. Continue cooking, turning occasionally, until the sugar and butter blend and the mixture is syrupy, about 2 minutes. Add the pecans to the frying pan and continue cooking and turning until the pears are well glazed and begin to brown and the pecans are glazed and heated through, about 3 minutes.
- Remove the greens from the refrigerator. Stir the dressing with your whisk and pour over the greens. Toss gently with large spoons. Spoon on the pear mixture and toss again. Serve immediately. Enjoy!

130. Pear Arugula And Pancetta Salad Recipe

Serving: 6 | Prep: | Cook: 5mins | Ready in:

Ingredients

- Vinaigrette:
- 2 T champagne vinegar
- 2 T mild honey
- 1 T Meyer lemon juice (a tad less regular lemon juice if Meyers are not available)
- 1/4 + salt
- 1/4 + coarsely ground black pepper

- 5 - 6 T high-quality extra virgin olive oil (probably not the kind you cook with but the one you save to finish off special dishes)
- For the salad:
- 4 oz thinly sliced (or tiny diced) pancetta
- 2 T olive oil (for cooking pancetta)
- 2 firm, but ripe, pears
- 5 - 6 c baby arugula or regular arugula torn into smaller pieces
- 4 - 5 oz ricotta salata or fresh parmesan (or percorino or other sharp, nutty hard cheese)

Direction

- For the Vinaigrette:
- Whisk together the vinegar, honey, lemon juice, salt and pepper in a salad bowl. Add oil in a slow stream, whisking until combined together.
- For the salad:
- Cook pancetta in the 2 T olive oil over moderate heat, stirring and turning frequently until just crisp, about 5 minutes. Transfer to paper towels to drain. The pancetta will crisp up more as it cools so don't overcook.
- Half pears lengthwise, core and cut into 1/4-inch slices.
- Add pears to dressing along with arugula, cheese and pancetta, tossing to coat.

---

131. Pear Blue Cheese And Candied Pecan Salad Recipe

Serving: 4 | Prep: | Cook: | Ready in:

Ingredients

- 1 Bartlett, Bosc, Comice or Red Anjou pear, peeled, seeded and sliced
- 2/3 cup candied pecan halves (or walnuts)
- 6 cups baby salad greens including baby spinach
- 1/2 cup blue cheese, crumbled
- 1/2 cup extra virgin olive oil
- 2 Tbsp. apple cider vinegar

- 1 teas. Dijon mustard
- 2 Tbsp. maple syrup

Direction

- Place baby salad greens in large, low salad bowl or plate. Arrange pear slices on top. Scatter with candied nuts and blue cheese.
- Combine oil, vinegar, mustard and maple syrup. Whisk thoroughly and lightly dress salad. Pass remaining dressing when serving salad.

---

132. Pear BlueCheese And Pecan Salad Recipe

Serving: 6 | Prep: | Cook: | Ready in:

Ingredients

- 1/2 cup pecans
- 1/4 cup white sugar
- 1/4 cup red wine vinegar
- 1 1/2 tsp sugar
- 1 tbs Dijon mustard
- 1/2 tsp salt
- 1/2 tsp minced garlic
- 1/8 tsp fresh ground pepper
- 3 tbs olive oil
- 1 head romaine lettuce, washed, trimmed and torn into bite-size pieces
- 3 pears, cored and chopped
- 2 ounces blue cheese, crumbled
- 1 small red onion, thinly sliced

Direction

- In small skillet over medium heat, stir pecans and 1/4 cup sugar
- Continue stirring gently until sugar has melted and caramelized the pecans.
- Transfer pecans onto a sheet of waxed paper.
- Allow to cool and break into pieces.
- In a small bowl, combine vinegar, 1 1/2 tsp sugar, mustard, garlic, salt and pepper.

- Slowly whisk in the olive oil.
- In a large bowl, layer lettuce, pears, blue cheese and onion.
- Pour dressing over salad, sprinkle with pecans and serve immediately.
- Dietary information per serving:
- Serving size 1 1/2 cups
- Calories: 260
- Protein: 5g
- Carbohydrates: 27g
- Fat: 17 g
- Cholesterol: 5 g
- Sodium: 400 mg
- Fiber: 4g

133.   Pear Cranberry Salad Toss Recipe

Serving: 4 | Prep: | Cook: |Ready in:

Ingredients

- 10 ounces mixed salad greens
- 2 medium pears sliced
- 1 cup pecan halves toasted
- 1 cup sweetened dried cranberries
- 1/2 cup sliced green onions
- 1/2 cup raspberry vinaigrette

Direction

- Toss greens, pears, pecans, cranberries and onions in large bowl.
- Add dressing then toss to coat and serve immediately.

134.   Pear Pecan And Shrimp Salad Recipe

Serving: 8 | Prep: | Cook: 5mins |Ready in:

Ingredients

- 1 bag mixed salad greens
- 1 cucumber peeled, seeded, & diced
- 1 roma tomato diced
- 1/2 c shredded carrot
- 1/2 c red bell pepper diced
- 1/2 c red onion diced
- 1/2 c bleu cheese crumbles
- 1 pear diced
- 6 oz medium shrimp cooked and diced
- 1/2 c sugared pecans bits
- Your favorite raspberry vinegrette (I like Maple Valley Nonfat)

Direction

- Make the sugar pecans by melting a teaspoon of butter in a small pan. Add the pecan pieces and heat until hot. Sprinkle with 1 T sugar and 1/8 teaspoon cinnamon. Remove pecans when the sugar melts. Cool.
- Diced all the vegetables and fruit about the same size.
- Toss the shrimp, vegetables, and fruit with the greens and the raspberry vinaigrette.
- Top with the bleu cheese and sugared pecan bits.
- We like shrimp or chicken if we eat this as a main dish; otherwise, we leave the meat out if it is a side dish.

135.   Pear Salad OR PineappleORPeaches Recipe

Serving: 8 | Prep: | Cook: 30mins |Ready in:

Ingredients

- 1 can pears, halves
- mayo
- cheddar cheese, shredded
- lettuce
- cherries

Direction

- On a large platter, put lettuce leaves, enough for each slice of fruit.
- Place a slice of fruit on the lettuce.
- Put a tsp. of mayo in the hole on the fruit.
- Put cheese on top of mayo.
- Put a cherry on top.
- Chill until ready to serve.

136.   Pear Salad Recipe

Serving: 4 | Prep: | Cook: |Ready in:

Ingredients

- 1 large cans of pears
- Finely grated cheddar cheese to taste
- lettuce (you can use any kind of lettuce but I prefer green leaf)
- Mayonaise

Direction

- Create a bed of lettuce in 4 salad plates or on a platter
- Place drained pears on the lettuce with cut side up
- Top with the finely grated cheddar cheese
- Top the cheese with a dollop of mayonnaise
- Serve
- ***
****
- My husband does not like mayonnaise so he has his dry and loves it.

137.   Pear Salad With Brie Recipe

Serving: 4 | Prep: | Cook: 15mins |Ready in:

Ingredients

- 2 C baby greens

- 2 medium to large pears (use red pears)
- fairly firm brie cheese , well chilled
- lemon juice
- olive oil
- good quality white wine vinegar

Direction

- Slice the pears thin & toss in a bowl with lemon juice to prevent discoloring.
- Drain & toss again with 4 T white wine vinegar.
- Put 1/2 C greens on each of 4 plates.
- Divide pear slices among 4 plates & drizzle with olive oil.
- Remove cheese from refrigerator & slice thinly with a serrated knife. Arrange sliced cheese over the pear mixture. Use as much as you like but don't overwhelm the pears, just accent them with the cheese.
- Taste & add more wine vinegar if needed.

138.   Pear Salad With Red Wine Vinaigrette Recipe

Serving: 12 | Prep: | Cook: 10mins |Ready in:

Ingredients

- 2 tablespoons extra-virgin olive oil
- 2 tablespoons red wine vinegar
- 1/2 teaspoon sugar
- 1/2 teaspoon minced garlic
- 1/4 teaspoon paprika
- 1/4 teaspoon dry mustard
- 1/8 teaspoon salt
- Pinch of dried basil
- Pinch of cayenne pepper
- 5 cups mixed salad greens
- 4 cups torn romaine lettuce
- 2 1/2 cups cubed Asian pear (about 1 large)
- 2 cups chopped Granny Smith apple (about 1 large)
- 1/2 cup thinly sliced red onion

- 1/4 cup (1 ounce) crumbled goat cheese

Direction

- Combine first 9 ingredients in a bowl, stirring with a whisk.
- Combine salad greens, romaine lettuce, Asian pear, apple, and red onion in a large bowl. Drizzle with vinaigrette, and toss well to coat. Sprinkle with crumbled goat cheese.

---

139. Pear Spinach Salad Recipe

Serving: 2 | Prep: | Cook: |Ready in:

Ingredients

- 2 cups fresh spinach
- 1 cup fresh pear dices
- 4 oz goat gouda

Direction

- Combine and enjoy
- Twice as much pear as Gouda makes a nice balance
- Adding marinated chicken, beef or tofu for a meal.

---

140. Pear Waldorf Salad Recipe

Serving: 4 | Prep: | Cook: |Ready in:

Ingredients

- Dressing: 2 T. reduced fat sour cream
- 1 T. light mayo
- 1 t. fresh lemon juice
- 1/8 t. salt
- Salad: 2 c. coarsely chopped bartlett pears-- about 2 pears

- 1 c. small seeless red grapes
- 2 T. chopped walnut

Direction

- Combine the first 4 ingredients in a small bowl; stir until smooth.
- Combine pear, grapes, walnuts and mayo mixture in a large bowl; toss gently

---

141. Pear Walnut And Blue Cheese Salad With Cranberry Vinaigrette Recipe

Serving: 6 | Prep: | Cook: 30mins |Ready in:

Ingredients

- Vinaigrette:
- 1/2 cup canned whole-berry cranberry sauce
- 1/4 cup fresh orange juice (about 1 orange)
- OR instead of above, I have used frozen natural cranberry orange sauce in freezer section near frozen fruit.
- 1 tablespoon olive oil
- 2 tablespoons balsamic vinegar
- 1 teaspoon sugar
- 1 teaspoon minced peeled fresh ginger
- 1/4 teaspoon salt
- Salad:
- 18 Bibb lettuce leaves (about 2 heads)
- 2 cups sliced peeled pear (about 2 pears)
- 2 tablespoons fresh orange juice
- 1 cup (1/8-inch-thick) slices red onion, separated into rings
- 1/3 cup (2 ounces) crumbled blue cheese
- 2 tablespoons coarsely chopped walnuts, toasted

Direction

- To prepare the vinaigrette, place the first 7 ingredients in a medium bowl; stir well with a whisk.

- To prepare the salad, divide the lettuce leaves evenly among 6 salad plates.
- Toss pear with 2 tablespoons orange juice.
- Divide pear and onion evenly among leaves.
- Top each serving with about 1 tablespoon cheese and 1 teaspoon walnuts.
- Drizzle each serving with about 2 1/2 tablespoons vinaigrette.
- CALORIES 148(38% from fat); FAT 6.3g (sat 1.8g,mono 2.5g,poly 1.5g); PROTEIN 2.7g; CHOLESTEROL 5mg; CALCIUM 60mg; SODIUM 205mg; FIBER 2.4g; IRON 0.4mg; CARBOHYDRATE 22.3g

142.   Pear Amp Smoked Turkey Salad Recipe

Serving: 4 | Prep: | Cook: |Ready in:

Ingredients

- 2 cups of baby spring greens
- 1 head of romaine chopped (about 2 cups)
- 1 pack of hydroponic spinach leaves (2 cups)
- 1 large bunch of green onions, diced
- 1/2 cup of chopped toasted pecans
- 2 red pears, cored and sliced thin or chunked
- 1 1/2 cups of smoked turkey, cut in a chunky dice
- Dressing:
- 1/2 cup of best mayonnaise
- 1/2 cup of whole berry cranberry sauce
- squeeze of one fresh lemon
- generous squeeze from the honey bear
- salt and pepper to taste

Direction

- Dice onions, chop pecans, chop pears, chop turkey.
- In a large bowl, mix the washed and dried greens. Add the other ingredients.
- Mix dressing with a fork, taste add salt and pepper to taste.
- Pour over salad, toss and eat right away.

- Feeds four generously.

143.   Pear And Walnut Salad Recipe

Serving: 4 | Prep: | Cook: 15mins |Ready in:

Ingredients

- 1 Comice pear,cored and thinly sliced
- 1 bartlett pear,cored and thinly sliced
- 1/4 c crumbled blue cheese
- 1/4 c walnuts,toasted and coarsely chopped
- 6 Tbs walnut oil
- 1/4 c pear liqueur or pear nectar
- 1 Tbs Walnut-Dijon mustard or Dijon-style mustard

Direction

- Arrange pear slices on four salad plates. Sprinkle cheese and walnuts.
- For dressing: Whisk together oil, liqueur and mustard. Season to taste with pepper. Drizzle 2 Tbs dressing on each salad. Cover and store remaining dressing up to 3 days; serve with spinach salad or cut up fruit.

144.   Pear Walnut Salad Recipe

Serving: 2 | Prep: | Cook: 10mins |Ready in:

Ingredients

- 3 tablespoons pear nectar
- 1 tablespoon seasoned rice vinegar
- 2 teaspoons olive oil
- 1/8 teaspoon coarsely ground black pepper
- 2 cups torn mixed salad greens
- 1/2 medium pear, cored and thinly sliced
- 1/4 small red onion, thinly sliced and separated into rings
- 2 tablespoons chopped walnuts, toasted

Direction

- For vinaigrette:
- In a small bowl, whisk together pear nectar, vinegar, oil, and pepper. Set aside.
- Arrange the lettuce on two salad plates. Top with pear, red onion, and walnuts. Drizzle with the vinaigrette. Makes 2 servings.

---

145.   Pears Pasta And Pecan Salad Recipe

Serving: 8 | Prep: | Cook: 10mins | Ready in:

Ingredients

- pasta Ingredients:
- 4 ounces (1 cup) uncooked dried gemelli (double twist pasta) or small pasta shells
- salad dressing Ingredients:
- 1/4 cup sour cream
- 1 teaspoon freshly grated lime peel
- 3 tablespoons lime juice
- 3 tablespoons olive or vegetable oil
- 2 tablespoons honey
- Salad Ingredients:
- 1/4 cup coarsely chopped pecans, toasted
- 2 ribs (1 cup) celery, sliced
- 1 medium pear, sliced, quartered
- 1 medium apple, sliced, quartered
- 2 tablespoons chopped green onions

Direction

- Cook gemelli according to package directions. Rinse with cold water; drain.
- Meanwhile, combine all salad dressing ingredients in small bowl.
- Just before serving, toss together cooked pasta and all remaining salad ingredients in large bowl. Drizzle with dressing; toss gently to coat.

---

146.   Persimmon Pear And Pomegranite Salad Recipe

Serving: 6 | Prep: | Cook: 8mins | Ready in:

Ingredients

- 1/2 cup pecan halves (2 ounces)
- 1 tablespoon red wine vinegar or passion fruit vinegar if you can find it
- 2 tablespoons chardonnay (white wine) vinegar
- 2 tablespoons pomegranite juice
- 1 tablespoon walnut or hazelnut oil
- 4 tablespoons extra-virgin olive oil or grapeseed oil
- salt and freshly ground pepper
- 1 small heads of frisée, torn
- 3 cups fresh mixed baby greens
- ½ cup pomegranate seeds
- 1-2 Fuyu persimmon, thinly sliced crosswise
- 1-2 red bartlett pear--halved, cored and thinly sliced
- handful of dried cranberries (optional)

Direction

- Preheat the oven to 375°.
- Spread the pecans in a pie plate and toast for 8 minutes, or until golden and fragrant.
- Let the nuts cool, then coarsely chop. Be sure to not skip toasting the pecans, because it makes them taste a lot better.
- In a small bowl, whisk together the vinegar, walnut oil and olive oil; season with salt and pepper.
- Can also put in a dressing shaker to serve.
- In a large bowl, toss the greens and frisée with the persimmon and pears.
- Add the vinaigrette and toss.
- Transfer the salad to a platter, garnish with the pecans, dried cranberries and pomegranate seeds and serve.

147. Raggedy Ann Salad Recipe

Serving: 1 | Prep: | Cook: 20mins | Ready in:

Ingredients

- 1 canned peach OR pear half (for the body)
- 1 piece curly lettuce (for her skirt)
- 1/2 hard-boiled egg, cut length-wise (for her head)
- 1 slice of American cheese, cut into thin strips (for her hair)
- 4 small celery ribs (legs and arms)
- 1 black olive, or marachino cherry, cut in half (for the shoes)
- 1 golden raisin (for her nose)
- 3 dark raisins (eyes and buttons)
- 1 marachino cherry (her mouth)
- Small dab of mayo (for "glue")

Direction

- Place the drained peach or pear half cut-side down in the center of a dinner plate. With a paper towel, pat the top of the fruit dry. Tuck the lettuce leaf under the bottom edge of the fruit for her skirt. Slide 2 celery ribs under the lettuce for the legs, and put the "shoes" in place. Place the other 2 celery ribs on each side of the fruit/body for her arms.
- Place the egg half at the top of the fruit for her head. Arrange the sliced cheese around the head for her hair.
- You'll be attaching the buttons (on the body) and the face features using a tiny dab of mayo to hold them in place. With a paper towel, dry the cherry so that cherry juice doesn't run on the egg; then slice the cherry so you have a "smile" shape. Cut small pieces from one dark raisin for the eyes, so they're smaller than the whole raisin used for the nose.

148. Roasted Beet Pistachio And Pear Salad Recipe

Serving: 2 | Prep: | Cook: 60mins | Ready in:

Ingredients

- 2 beets (about 3/4 pound)
- 1c asian pear or ripe pear, cubed
- 1/4c celery, chopped
- 2T pistachios, chopped
- 3T lemon juice, fresh
- 1T honey
- 1/2t brown sugar
- 1/4t black pepper
- Dash of salt
- Dash of ground red pepper
- 2 curly leaf lettuce leaves (optional)

Direction

- Preheat oven to 425*.
- Leave root and 1" of stem on beets; scrub with a brush. Place beets in a small baking dish. Bake at 425* for 50 minutes or until tender. Cool. Trim off beet roots and stems; rub off skins. Dice beets.
- Combine beets, pears, celery, and pistachios in a medium bowl.
- Combine juice and next 5 ingredients, stirring well with a whisk. Drizzle over beet mixture, tossing gently to coat. Serve at room temperature or chilled over lettuce leaves, if desired.
- 153 calories; 22% from fat

149. Roasted Pear Salad Recipe

Serving: 4 | Prep: | Cook: 50mins | Ready in:

Ingredients

- * 4 bosc pears, halved, cored, sliced in eighths
- * 8 shallots, peeled, halved

- * 3 tablespoons chilled butter, cut into small pieces
- * 6 tablespoons apple cider
- * 1/4 cup honey
- * 2 teaspoons fresh lemon juice
- * 1 large clove garlic, minced
- * 2 tablespoons raspberry vinegar
- * 1 tablespoon basil
- * 1/2 cup grapeseed oil
- * 1/2 teaspoon salt
- * 1/2 teaspoon freshly ground pepper
- * 1/4 cup port wine
- * 8 cups salad greens
- * 1/4 cup crumbled blue cheese
- * 1/4 cup toasted walnut pieces
- Dir

Direction

- Preheat oven to 400 F.
- Place pears and shallots in a 13 x 9-inch baking dish coated with cooking spray; dot with butter.
- Combine cider, honey and lemon juice in a small saucepan.
- Bring to a boil, and pour over the pear mixture.
- Cover and bake for 20 minutes.
- Uncover and bake an additional 30 minutes or until the pears are tender, basting occasionally.
- Remove from oven and transfer pears and shallots to bowl; set aside. Reserve pear liquid.
- Combine garlic, pear liquid, vinegar, basil, oil, salt, pepper and port in the work bowl of food processor.
- Process until blended.
- Arrange salad greens on 4 serving plates.
- Divide pears and shallots over greens.
- Sprinkle with blue cheese and walnuts.
- Drizzle with port vinaigrette.

150. Roasted Pear And Toasted Goat Cheese Salad Recipe

Serving: 4 | Prep: | Cook: 35mins | Ready in:

Ingredients

- 2 pears, unpeeled
- 3/4 cup apple juice or apple cider
- 3 tablespoons brown sugar
- 1 tablespoon white wine vinegar
- 1 tablespoon extra-virgin olive oil
- salt and pepper, to taste
- One 5-ounce package spring mix salad greens
- 1 tablespoon toasted chopped walnuts
- 2 tablespoons dried cranberries
- 3 to 4 ounces goat cheese (log form)
- 1 egg white
- 1 tablespoon water
- 1/3 cup panko crumbs

Direction

- Preheat oven to 375 degrees.
- Cut pears in half and remove core and seeds from each pear.
- Cut each half in half again and place in a baking dish.
- Combine apple juice and brown sugar.
- Stir until brown sugar has dissolved; pour over pears.
- Bake the pears 20 to 30 minutes, or until tender, basting occasionally with the apple juice mixture.
- Use a slotted spoon and remove pears to a plate to cool slightly.
- Reserve 1/4 cup apple juice mixture.
- Place reserved 1/4 cup apple juice mixture and white wine vinegar in small bowl. Whisk in olive oil until blended.
- Season with salt and pepper.
- Place spring greens in salad bowl and toss with dressing.
- Divide among four plates.
- Sprinkle evenly with walnuts and cranberries.
- Slice goat cheese into 4 slices.

- Whisk together egg white and water.
- Dip goat cheese into egg white mixture and coat both sides evenly with panko crumbs.
- Spray a small nonstick skillet with nonstick spray coating, then heat over medium high heat.
- Toast goat cheese rounds about 30 seconds per side.
- Serve warm on the side of the salad.
- Place pears alongside green

151. Roasted Red Onion And Pear Salad Recipe

Serving: 6 | Prep: | Cook: 25mins | Ready in:

Ingredients

- 2Tbs orange juice
- 1Tbs lemon juice
- 1tsp Dijon mustard
- 1tsp honey
- 1/4tsp chopped fresh thyme leaves
- 6Tbs vegetable oil or olive oil
- salt and ground black pepper
- 1 red onion,cut in 1" wedges,with root end intact
- 1 head bibb lettuce
- 1(6oz) bag baby spinach(about 8 cups)
- 1 ripe pear,cored and cut in 1" chunks
- 1/2c crumbled goat cheese
- 1c smokehouse almonds,chopped coarse
- 1/4c dried cranberries

Direction

- Adjust oven rack to middle position and heat to 400.
- Whisk orange and lemon juices, mustard, honey and thyme together in med. bowl. Gradually whisk in 4 Tbs oil. Season with salt and pepper.
- Toss onion wedges with remaining 2 Tbs oil, 1/4tsp salt and 1/4tsp pepper. Transfer to baking sheet and roast until brown and soft, 25

mins, flipping wedges halfway through cooking. Cool 15 mins.
- Divide Bibb lettuce leaves among salad plates. Toss spinach with 1/4c dressing in large bowl. Divide spinach among plates. Arrange roasted onions, pear, goat cheese, almonds and cranberries on top.
- Drizzle with remaining dressing and serve.

152. Rocket Pear Cheese Salad Recipe

Serving: 4 | Prep: | Cook: | Ready in:

Ingredients

- 1 bunch rocket, trimmed - or lettuce of your choice
- 4 slices prosciutto, fried until crisp, then crumbled
- 2 pears, cored and sliced
- 4 oz blue cheese, crumbled - I use gorgonzola
- 1/2 cup black olives
- Dressing:
- 1/4 cup olive oil
- 1 tblsp red wine vinegar
- 1 tblsp white wine vinegar
- 2 tsp Dijon or grain mustard
- salt and black pepper (freshly ground), to taste

Direction

- Arrange rocket, crumbled prosciutto, pear, cheese and olives in a salad bowl.
- To prepare dressing, whisk ingredients together.
- Pour over salad just before serving. Serve with bread for a light lunch or as a meal accompaniment.

153. Salad With Pears Walnuts Cranberry Vinaigrette Recipe

Serving: 6 | Prep: | Cook: | Ready in:

Ingredients

- For Vinaigrette:
- 1/2 cup whole berry cranberry sauce
- 1/4 cup fresh orange juice-about 1 orange
- 1 Tbls. olive oil
- 2 Tbls. balsamic vinegar
- 1/2 tsp. sugar (or more if needed)
- 1 tsp. peeled fresh minced ginger
- 1/4 tsp. sea salt
- For Salad:
- 18 romaine leaves (about 2)
- 2 pears peeled and sliced
- 2 Tbls. orange juice
- 1 cup sliced red onion
- 1/3 cup crumbled blue cheese
- 2 Tbls. toasted walnuts coarsely chopped

Direction

- For Vinaigrette:
- Place all ingredients in a medium sized bowl and whisk well.
- Salad:
- Divide lettuce leaves evenly on 6 salad plates
- Toss pears with 2 tbsp. orange juice
- Divide pears and onions on plates
- Top each serving with 1 Tbsp. cheese and walnuts
- Top with 2 1/2 tbsp. vinaigrette.....Enjoy

154. Seasonal French Pears Baby Salad Greens Toasted Pine Nuts With Gorgonzola Recipe

Serving: 2 | Prep: | Cook: | Ready in:

Ingredients

- 1/3 cup pine nuts (also called pignoli)
- 2 French pears, thinly sliced
- 1 pound baby mixed greens
- 1/4 lb. gorgonzola
- ------------------------
- Dressing
- ---------------------
- 1 tablespoon shallots, chopped
- 1 1/2 tablespoons Dijon mustard
- 2 tablespoons honey
- 1/3 cup chopped tarragon
- 1/4 cup red wine vinegar
- salt & freshly ground pepper
- 2/3 cup olive oil
- PREP WORK Chop the shallots and tarragon. Assemble the rest of the ingredients together

Direction

- DRESSING

155. Spinach Pear Salad With Citrus Dressing Recipe

Serving: 4 | Prep: | Cook: | Ready in:

Ingredients

- 1/2lb thick cut bacon, fried crisp and crumbled
- 1 bag fresh baby spinach
- 2 eggs, hard cooked and sliced
- 3oz colby or mild cheddar cheese, cubed or matchsticked
- fresh ground black pepper
- *dressing*
- 1/2 cup mayonnaise
- 3T orange juice, fresh
- 1t nutmeg

Direction

- In large salad bowl, combine all ingredients other than black pepper and dressing ingredients and toss until just combined.

- Combine dressing ingredients and add to salad, tossing lightly and adding pepper to top just prior to serving.
- Try serving with the orange wedges and toasted garlic pumpernickel bread.

156. Spinach Pear And Shaved Parmesan Salad Recipe

Serving: 8 | Prep: | Cook: | Ready in:

Ingredients

- 8 cups lightly packed baby spinah leaves, stemmed, rinsed and dried (you can use canned pears)
- 2 bosc pears (do not peel) quartered, cored and cut into long this slices
- 1/2 cup (2oz.) coarsley grated Parmigiano-Reggiano
- Dressing:
- 1/2 cup extra virgin olive oil
- 2 Tbs. balsamic vinegar
- 2 tsp. whole-grain mustard
- 1tsp. sugar
- 1 tsp. salt
- freshly ground pepper

Direction

- Place the spinach and pears in a large serving bowl. Scatter the cheese on top.
- To make the dressing
- In a small jar with a tight lid, combine the olive oil, vinegar, mustard, sugar, salt, and pepper to taste.
- Taste and adjust the seasonings.
- Pour the dressing over the salad and toss gently.
- Serve immediately

157. Spinach Salad With Candied Pecans Pears And Brie Recipe

Serving: 8 | Prep: | Cook: 15mins | Ready in:

Ingredients

- 1/3 c. pecan halves
- 3 Tbsp. icing sugar
- 1/4 tsp. cinnamon
- 1/8 tsp. allspice
- 1/8 tsp. nutmeg
- 2 Tbsp. orange juice concentrate, thawed
- 2 Tbsp. olive oil
- 1 Tbsp. balsamic vinegar
- 1 tsp. minced garlic
- 1/2 tsp. honey
- 1/2 tsp. Dijon mustard
- 8 c. baby spinach leaves
- 1 c. radicchio
- 1 large ripe pear, peeled, cored and diced
- 2 oz. brie, diced

Direction

- Preheat oven to 350*. Spray baking sheet with cooking oil.
- Rinse the pecans with cold water. Drain, but don't let them dry. Combine the icing sugar, cinnamon, allspice and nutmeg in a small bowl. Dip the pecans in the sugar mixture, coating well. Spread on the baking sheet.
- Bake for 15 minutes in the center of oven. Remove and cool. When cool enough to handle, coarsely chop them.
- Combine the spinach, radicchio pear and brie in a large serving bowl.
- Whisk together the orange juice concentrate, oil, vinegar, garlic, honey and mustard in small bowl. Pour over salad and toss to coat. Garnish with candied pecans.

158.   Spinach And Pear Salad Recipe

Serving: 46 | Prep: | Cook: | Ready in:

Ingredients

- 1/4 red onion, thinly sliced
- 2 tablespoons Dijon mustard
- 2 tablespoons red wine vinegar
- 2 tablespoons water
- 1 tablespoon olive oil
- 1 tablespoon honey
- 1/2 teaspoon kosher salt
- 1/2 teaspoon freshly ground black pepper
- 5 cups baby spinach (about 5 ounces)
- 1 medium bosc pear, quartered and thinly sliced

Direction

- Place onion in a small bowl of ice water and let sit for 10 minutes.
- Meanwhile, place mustard, vinegar, water, oil, honey, salt, and pepper in a medium nonreactive bowl and whisk until combined.
- Strain onion from ice water, pat dry, and place in a large nonreactive bowl. Add spinach, pear, and 3 tablespoons of the dressing and toss until evenly coated.

159.   Stacked Spinach And Pear Salad With Blue Cheese Recipe

Serving: 4 | Prep: | Cook: 15mins | Ready in:

Ingredients

- 2 pears(core removed)
- 4c baby spinach(washed)
- 8Tbs crumbled blue cheese
- 4Tbs olive oil
- 4tsp balsamic vinegar
- salt and pepper to taste

Direction

- Thinly slice pear into 1/8' slices horizontal and keep each pear together to retain its shape.
- Arrange alternate layers of half a pear and 1c spinach leaves per salad to make a stack. Sprinkle each salad with 2 Tbs. of blue cheese, and season with salt and pepper.
- Drizzle each salad with 1 Tbsp. olive oil and 1 tsp. vinegar just before serving.
- Bartlett pears are great for this, red or yellow.

160.   Steak And Pear Salad Recipe

Serving: 4 | Prep: | Cook: 10mins | Ready in:

Ingredients

- 1 pound of Top sirloin or flank steak
- 5 oz of mixed greens
- 1 Can of Chick peas, drained and rinsed
- 1/4 lb of blue cheese
- 1 Ripe yet Firm pear
- 6 Tablespoons of olive oil
- 2 Tablespoons of lemon juice
- 1/4 tsp of salt
- Fresh cracked black pepper

Direction

- Preheat Your Grill to High (Indoor or Outdoor).
- Rub the steak with oil and salt on both sides.
- While the grill is heating - wash the greens and drain and rinse the chick peas. Crumble the blue cheese into bite size pieces.
- Cut the pear in half and scoop out the core. Then quarter and slice it into thin 'salad' sized pieces.
- Reduce the heat of the grill to medium - and cook the steak for about 5 minutes a side to medium-rare or medium. Let it rest for 5 minutes while you prepare the salad.

- Whisk the Olive Oil slowly into the lemon juice. After the oil is all mixed in, whisk in the salt and fresh cracked pepper.
- Thinly slice the steak across the grain and top the salad with it.

---

161.   Sweet Cranberry Pear Salad Recipe

Serving: 2 | Prep: | Cook: |Ready in:

Ingredients

- 6 cups torn mixed salad greens
- 3 medium pears, cut into 3/4-inch cubes
- 1/2 cup dried cranberries
- 1/2 cup PLANTERS walnut pieces, toasted
- 1 cup Hawaiian bread croutons
- 1/2 cup Miracle Whip Dressing
- 1 env. GOOD SEASONS Italian dressing Mix
- 1/4 cup white vinegar
- 3 Tbsp. water

Direction

- TOSS greens with pears, cranberries and walnuts in large salad bowl; top with the croutons. Set aside.
- MIX MIRACLE WHIP, dressing mix, vinegar and water.
- DRIZZLE over the salad just before serving.
- Serving Suggestion
- Serve with 3 oz. of your favorite cooked lean fish, meat or poultry to round out the meal.
- How to Make Croutons
- Preheat oven to 350°F. Cut Hawaiian bread loaf into 1-inch-thick slices. Brush both sides of each slice lightly with olive oil; cut into 1-inch cubes. Spread into 15x10x1-inch baking pan. Bake 10 to 12 min. or until lightly browned, stirring occasionally. Cool. Store in airtight container at room temperature until ready to use.
- Substitute

- Substitute 1 bag (10 oz.) torn spinach leaves for the mixed salad greens and/or dried cherries for the cranberries.

---

162.   Tossed Salad With Pears Recipe

Serving: 8 | Prep: | Cook: |Ready in:

Ingredients

- 1/3 cup pecan halves
- 1/2 tsp cinnamon
- 5 cups torn mixed salad greens, your favorite.
- 1 large pear, hard, sliced into thin wedges.
- 1/2 cup colby cheese, crumbled.
- 1/4 cup fresh cranberries, chopped
- 1/3 cup Spicy Italian dressing

Direction

- Place pecans in microwave plate sprayed with cooking spray. Sprinkle with cinnamon, toss to coat. Spread out and microwave for 1.5 minutes on HIGH. Stir every 30 seconds.
- Toss greens, pears, cheese and cranberries in a large bowl.
- Add pecans and dressing just before serving.

---

163.   Tuna And Pear Salad Recipe

Serving: 2 | Prep: | Cook: |Ready in:

Ingredients

- 6 oz. tuna
- 1/2 onion
- 1/2 pear-very ripe
- grape tomatoes (as many as you like)
- 1 Toe minced garlic (i used purple garlic)
- 1 TBS olive oil

- 3 TBS balsamic vinegar
- Course ground black pepper
- 2 TBS Crumbled feta cheese

Direction

- Chop onion very fine
- Mince garlic
- Slice tomatoes if you like
- Cube the pear
- Add all ingredients to tuna and toss

---

164. Tuna Waldorf Salad With Pear In English Recipe

Serving: 2 | Prep: | Cook: | Ready in:

Ingredients

- 1 can (5oz) white tuna in water
- 1/4 large pear (or apple)
- 1/4 cup (1oz) chopped walnuts, raw (toasted if you prefer)
- 1/4 cup red onion, diced
- 2 Tbsp. low fat mayonnaise
- 1 Tbsp. lemon juice
- 2 lettuce leaves - for serving

Direction

- Drain the tuna.
- Chop onion and walnuts, cut pear in cubes.
- Mix mayo and lemon juice.
- Put all the ingredients in a bowl and mix all together.
- Chill the salad before serving. Serve on a lettuce leaf.

---

165. Waldorf Pear Salad Recipe

Serving: 4 | Prep: | Cook: | Ready in:

Ingredients

- 1/4 cup of mayonnaise
- 1/4 cup of sour cream
- 1/3 cup of blue cheese crumbled
- 1 cup of celery
- 1/2 cup of toasted walnuts chopped
- 1 large can of pears, drained and diced
- or two pears, cored and chopped

Direction

- Mix the mayonnaise, sour cream and blue cheese.
- Add celery and nuts.
- Fold in diced pears.
- Chill and serve.

---

166. Apple And Pear Salad Recipe

Serving: 23 | Prep: | Cook: 60mins | Ready in:

Ingredients

- 1 apple
- 1 pear
- 2 tbs.lemon juice
- 1/4 cup mayo
- 1/4 cup plain yogurt
- 3 cups shredded cabbage
- 1/4 cup finely chopped celery and onion
- 1/4 cup chopped pecans
- 1/4 cup raisins
- salt and pepper

Direction

- In a large glass bowl put chopped apple and pear with lemon juice
- Mix yogurt and mayo and add to apples and pears
- Add remaining ingredients and mix well
- Chill for 1 hr.

167. Pear And Duck Confit Salad Recipe

Serving: 4 | Prep: | Cook: 30mins |Ready in:

Ingredients

- 1 teaspoon Dijon mustard
- 1 tablespoon Sherry vinegar
- 5 tablespoons extra-virgin olive oil
- 2 tablespoons finely chopped shallot
- 1/2 cup pecans, coarsely chopped
- 2 confit duck legs
- 3 firm-ripe Anjou or bartlett pears (preferably red)
- 8 cups mixed greens, such as frisée(French curly endive), tender watercress sprigs, and baby spinach leaves
- 2 oz crumbled Roquefort or other blue cheese (1/2 cup), optional

Direction

- Preheat oven to 250°F.
- Whisk together mustard, vinegar, and salt and pepper to taste in a large bowl. Add 4 tablespoons oil in a slow stream, whisking until emulsified, then whisk in shallot.
- Heat remaining tablespoon oil in a 10-inch heavy skillet over moderate heat until hot but not smoking, then cook pecans, stirring, until golden brown. Transfer nuts with a slotted spoon to paper towels to drain, then season with salt.
- Heat skillet with any oil remaining in it over moderately high heat until hot but not smoking, then brown duck on all sides until crisp, about 5 minutes. Transfer to a cutting board and tear meat into bite-size pieces and discard bones. Keep duck warm, covered, on a baking sheet in oven.
- Halve and core pears and cut lengthwise into 1/4-inch-thick slices. Add pears, greens, duck, cheese, and nuts to dressing with salt and pepper to taste, then toss gently to combine.

168. Sweet And Savoury Salad With Pear And Blue Cheese Recipe

Serving: 1 | Prep: | Cook: |Ready in:

Ingredients

- 1/2 bartlett pear-sliced and cut into bite size pieces
- 1/4 green apple-shredded (soaked in orange juice to keep from turning brown)
- 1/2 an endive head-sliced
- small handful of bitter green such as baby arugula
- 2 TBSP crumbled blue cheese
- fresh cracked pepper from a mill
- dressing
- 2 TBSP balsamic vinegar
- 1 TBSP maple syrup (or honey or sugar)
- 1 clove of garlic-crushed
- regular olive oil (not virgin)-to taste-about 4-6 TBSP

Direction

- Combine all ingredients for dressing in a small jar or plastic container and shake until emulsified...about 2/3 oil and 1/3 other liquids. Set aside.
- Mix endive and arugula in a medium size bowl with shredded apple.
- Drizzle lightly with some dressing and toss gently, thoroughly coating each piece.
- Arrange pear on top and drizzle with about another 1 TBSP dressing.
- Add blue cheese and finish with fresh cracked pepper.
- Enjoy!
- *the reason not to use virgin olive oil is that the flavour is too heavy and will overpower the light taste of this salad.

Chapter 3: Awesome Fruit Salad Recipes

***

169.   APPLE ROTINI SALAD Recipe

Serving: 8 | Prep: | Cook: |Ready in:

Ingredients

- 3 tablespoons concentrated apple juice (you can get this frozen)
- 3 tablespoons light corn syrup
- 1 teaspoon cider vinegar
- 2 teaspoons firmly packed brown sugar
- 1/8 teaspoon garlic salt
- Dash pepper
- 1 package rotini noodles
- 2 cups chopped apples
- 2 cups shredded salad greens
- 1 cup of mandarin orange slices or strawberries when accessable
- 1/2 cup thin sliced celery
- 1/4 cup sliced green onions
- 2 tablespoons pine nuts

Direction

- Combine apple juice concentrate, corn syrup, vinegar, sugar, garlic salt and pepper.
- Cover and refrigerate.
- Cook the rotini according to package directions.
- Drain and cool thoroughly.
- In large mixing bowl combine rotini and remaining ingredients. Toss gently with apple juice dressing and serve immediately.

170.   Ambrosia Recipe

Serving: 0 | Prep: | Cook: 10mins |Ready in:

Ingredients

- 20 oz pineapple, drained
- 11 oz mandarin oranges, drained
- 1 1/2 cups grapes, cut in half
- 1 cup mini marshmallows
- 1 cup coconut
- 1/2 cup chopped nuts (I use pecans)
- 3/4 cup Cool Whip -- partially thawed
- 1/2 banana (per serving)

Direction

- Combine all the fruits (minus the banana), nuts, coconut, and marshmallows.
- Whip through the Cool Whip, then fold into the fruit mixture. Chill.
- Serve in a dish and stir into each dish half a sliced up banana into the mixture. (This prevents the banana from getting mushy or brown -- if you don't care mix it in at the beginning!)

171.   Antipasto Pasta Salad Recipe

Serving: 12 | Prep: | Cook: 30mins |Ready in:

Ingredients

- 1 pound Radiatori or fusilli pasta
- 1/4 pound genoa salami, chopped
- 1/4 pound pepperoni sausage, chopped
- 1/2 pound provolone cheese, diced
- 1 (6 ounce) can black olives, drained and sliced
- 1 (6 ounce) jar artichoke hearts, drained and cut in quarters
- 1 red bell pepper, diced
- 1 green bell pepper, chopped
- 1 medium sweet onion, diced
- 3 tomatoes, chopped

- 1 (.7 ounce) package dry Italian-style salad dressing mix*
- 3/4 cup extra virgin olive oil (no substitutions)
- 1/4 cup balsamic vinegar*
- 2 tablespoons dried oregano, crushed
- 1 tablespoon chopped fresh flat-leaf parsley parsley
- 2 tablespoons grated Asiago or romano cheese
- squeeze of fresh lemon juice
- salt and ground black pepper to taste

Direction

- Cook the pasta in a large pot of salted boiling water until al dente. Drain and shock pasta with cold water.
- In a large bowl, combine the pasta, salami, pepperoni, cheese, black olives, artichoke hearts, red bell pepper, green bell pepper, onion and tomatoes. Stir in the envelope of dressing mix*. Cover and refrigerate for at least one hour.
- To prepare the dressing, whisk together the olive oil, balsamic vinegar*, oregano, parsley, cheese, lemon juice, salt and pepper. Just before serving, pour dressing over the salad, and mix well.

---

172. Apple Almond Crunch Salad Recipe

Serving: 4 | Prep: | Cook: |Ready in:

Ingredients

- 1 cup tart apple cored and chopped
- 1/2 cup crumbled feta cheese
- 1/2 cup slivered almonds
- 1 cup raspberry vinaigrette salad dressing
- 10 ounce package mixed salad greens
- 1/4 cup sliced red onion
- 1/4 cup golden raisins

Direction

- In large salad bowl combine salad greens, almonds, cheese, apple, red onion and raisins.
- Toss to blend then apply salad dressing to individual servings.

---

173. Apple And Blue Cheese Salad Recipe

Serving: 6 | Prep: | Cook: |Ready in:

Ingredients

- 2 Tbs. Sherry-wine vinegar
- 1 Tbs. fresh-squeezed lemon Jucie
- 1 Tbs. honey
- 1/4 tsp. salt
- 1/4 tsp. black pepper
- 1/3 cup Extra-Virgin oilive Oil
- 10 cups mixed salad greens
- 4 ounces hard blue cheese, crumbled
- 3 large Red Delicious, Gala or Cortland apples, cored and cut into 3/4-inch cubes
- 2 ribs celery, sliced
- 1/2 red onion, sliced

Direction

- In medium-size bowl, whisk together vinegar, lemon juice, honey, salt and pepper.
- Gradually drizzle in olive oil while whisking until thick and well blended.
- In large bowl, toss together the salad greens, blue cheese, apples, celery and onion until well mixed. (I also like to toss in walnut pieces.)
- Drizzle dressing over top of salad; toss to evenly coat ingredients.
- If desired sprinkle with extra cheese.
- Serve immediately.

174.   Apple And Celery Salad Recipe

Serving: 4 | Prep: | Cook: |Ready in:

Ingredients

- 1/4 cup mayonnaise
- 2 tbls. Dijon mustard
- 2 tsp. cider vinegar1/2 tsp. sugar
- 2 tsp. tarragon, fresh (1/2 tsp. dried)
- salt and pepper to taste
- 2 tart apples, cored, peeled, and sliced into matchsticks
- 6 celery ribs, sliced into matchsticks

Direction

- Mix first 5 ingredients in mixing bowl until smooth
- Pour over apple and celery and mix until well combined

175.   Apple And Fennel Salad Recipe

Serving: 8 | Prep: | Cook: |Ready in:

Ingredients

- 1 large fennel bulb, stems and leaves
- 1 to 2 large red skinned crisp sweet apples
- chopped walnuts as desired
- light olive oil to moisten
- honey to taste
- salt and pepper

Direction

- Cut off root part of fennel, chop the bulb and stems finely (I used food processor) reserve the fringy leaves
- Chop the apple in the same consistency
- Mix apple and fennel together with some chopped walnuts

- Moisten all with olive oil
- Sweeten with honey
- Salt and pepper to taste
- Best serve the first one to 2 days, after that still great but loses some crispness
- Place in bowl and garish with fennel fronds
- Serve well chilled

176.   Apple And Walnut Salad Recipe

Serving: 8 | Prep: | Cook: |Ready in:

Ingredients

- 1 Large bag of spring mix
- 4 apples, washed & sliced
- 2 cups halved horizontally seedless red grapes
- 2 cups halved horizontally cherry or grape tomatoes
- 1/4 red onions, thinly sliced
- 4 oz glazed walnuts
- Balsamic Dressing - 1/4 cup balsamic vinegar, 1/4 cup fat-free, less-sodium chicken broth, 1 Tbsp frozen orange juice concentrate, thawed, 1 1/2 tsp sugar, 2 tsp extravirgin olive oil, 1 tsp Dijon mustard, 1/2 tsp salt, 1/4 tsp freshly ground black pepper, 1 tsp garlic,minced.

Direction

- To prepare vinaigrette, combine all ingredients, stirring with a whisk.
- To prepare salad, combine spring mix, apples, grape, tomato, onion in a large bowl.
- Right before serving, add walnut, drizzle with dressing; toss gently to coat. Serve immediately

177. Apple Apricot Salad Recipe

Serving: 4 | Prep: | Cook: | Ready in:

Ingredients

- 2/3 cup apricot nectar juice
- 1 small package instant dry vanilla pudding
- 2 cups peach slices drained
- 2 medium granny smith apples
- 2 medium red delicious apples
- 1 cup grapes red and green
- 1 cup pineapple

Direction

- In large bowl whisk together apricot juice and pudding mix.
- Cut peach slices in bite size pieces.
- Wash fresh fruit.
- Core apples and cut in bite size pieces.
- Add peaches, pineapple, apples and grapes to apricot mix then stir gently to coat.
- Chill well before serving.

178. Apple Avocado Beet Salad Recipe

Serving: 1 | Prep: | Cook: | Ready in:

Ingredients

- 2 Large beets, Cooked, peeled and thinly sliced
- ½ Cup cider vinaigrette
- mixed salad greens, rinsed, dried, and torn into bite-size pieces
- 1 small onion, cut into thin rings
- 1 apple, Peeled and thinly sliced
- ½ avocado, Cut in thin wedges
- ½ Cup walnuts, Chopped
- cider vinaigrette
- ¾ Cup apple cider
- ⅔ Cup cider vinegar
- ½ Cup oil

- ½ tsp. salt
- pepper
- 1 tsp. mustard
- ¼ tsp celery seed

Direction

- Combine beets and vinaigrette and let marinate at least half an hour, up to a full day.
- Shortly before serving, divide the greens among four luncheon-size plates.
- Drain beets and reserve dressing.
- Arrange layers of beet, onion, apple, and avocado on the greens and drizzle with reserved dressing.
- Sprinkle on the nuts and serve at once.
- For the dressing:
- Whisk everything together.

179. Apple Avocado Salad With Tangerine Dressing Recipe

Serving: 4 | Prep: | Cook: 10mins | Ready in:

Ingredients

- 1 (10 ounce) package baby greens
- 1/4 cup chopped red onion
- 1/2 cup chopped walnuts
- 1/3 cup crumbled blue cheese
- 2 teaspoons lemon zest
- 1 apple - peeled, cored and sliced
- 1 avocado - peeled, pitted and diced
- 4 mandarin oranges, juiced
- 1/2 lemon, juiced
- 1/2 teaspoon lemon zest
- 1 clove garlic, minced
- 2 tablespoons olive oil
- salt to taste

Direction

- In a large bowl, toss together the baby greens, red onion, walnuts, blue cheese, and lemon zest. Mix in the apple and avocado just before serving.

- In a container with a lid, mix the mandarin orange juice, lemon juice, lemon zest, garlic, olive oil, and salt. Drizzle over the salad as desired.

180.   Apple Bacon And Spinach Salad Recipe

Serving: 4 | Prep: | Cook: 10mins | Ready in:

Ingredients

- 6 slices bacon, cooked crispy, drained - save 1/2 of the bacon drippings
- 1 bag of baby spinach, thoroughly washed & spun dry
- 1 honey crisp apple, cored and sliced into thin wedges
- 1/4 cup finely diced red onion
- 1/4 cup sliced fresh mushrooms (shitakes work great)
- 2 teas. Dijon mustard
- 2 Tbsp. red wine vinegar
- 2 Tbsp. honey
- 3 Tbsp. extra virgin olive oil

Direction

- Rinse apple slices with a little water mixed with lemon juice to keep them from turning dark, drain. Combine apples, spinach and 4 slices of bacon, crumbled, in a salad bowl.
- In pan with reserved bacon drippings, turn to medium heat - when hot add onions and mushrooms, Cook until onion is barely tender. Remove from heat and add remaining 2 slices of bacon, crumbled. Stir to combine. Pour into a heatproof bowl. Add vinegar, Dijon mustard, honey and olive oil. Whisk to combine and lightly dress spinach-apple mixture. Toss and serve.

181.   Apple Banana Salad Recipe

Serving: 4 | Prep: | Cook: | Ready in:

Ingredients

- 2 medium red delicious apples diced
- 1 large banana halved lengthwise and sliced
- 1 cup celery thinly sliced
- 1/2 cup mayonnaise
- 4 teaspoons granulated sugar
- 1 tablespoon milk
- lettuce leaves

Direction

- Place apples, banana and celery in a medium bowl then set aside.
- In a small bowl mix mayonnaise, sugar and milk until smooth.
- Pour over apple mixture and toss until well coated then serve on lettuce leaves.

182.   Apple Camembert Spinach Salad Recipe

Serving: 6 | Prep: | Cook: 5mins | Ready in:

Ingredients

- 2 apples, cut into 1/2 inch wedges (I like granny smith)
- 2 tbls. maple syrup
- 4 cups fresh spinach
- 4 oz. camembert cheese (or Brie), cubed
- 1/4 cup pecan halves, toasted
- Dressing
- 2 tbls. apple cider or juice
- 2 tbls. canola oil
- 1 1/2 tbls. cider vinegar
- 1/2 tsp. Dijon mustard
- 1/2 clove garlic, finely chopped

Direction

- Preheat oven to broil
- Put apples on baking sheet and brush with maple syrup
- Broil at least 4 inches from heat for 3 minutes
- Flip and brush with remaining syrup
- Broil 3-5 minutes or until crisp tender
- In salad bowl, combine spinach, cheese, pecans and apples
- In saucepan, add dressing ingredients
- Bring to boil
- Pour over salad and serve immediately

---

183. Apple Chicken Salad With Garlic Blue Cheese Dressing Recipe

Serving: 4 | Prep: | Cook: 10mins | Ready in:

Ingredients

- 8 slices bacon
- 1 cup chopped pecans
- 4 cups torn romaine
- 1 cup finely chopped apple
- 2-1/2 cups shredded rotisserie chicken
- 1/2 small red onion thinly sliced
- 2 tablespoons crumbled blue cheese
- Dressing:
- 2 cups buttermilk
- 1 cup crumbled blue cheese
- 1 cup sour cream
- 1/4 cup mayonnaise
- 1/4 cup Dijon mustard
- 1 tablespoon lemon juice
- 3 cloves garlic chopped
- 1 teaspoon freshly ground black pepper

Direction

- Cook bacon in skillet over medium heat.
- Drain on paper towels reserving 2 tablespoons drippings in skillet.

- Add pecans to skillet and sauté until toasted.
- In large bowl toss greens with pecans, crumbled bacon and apple.
- Divide among four dinner plates and arrange chicken slices on top of each salad.
- Top each salad with onion and blue cheese and serve with dressing.
- To make dressing combine all ingredients in blender and process until smooth.

---

184. Apple Craisin Lettuce Salad Recipe

Serving: 8 | Prep: | Cook: | Ready in:

Ingredients

- 2 pkgs. lettuce (romaine and spring greens etc.)
- 1 pkg. or 1 1/2 cups craisins
- 1 1/2 cups cashew pieces
- 1 large apple chopped
- 8 oz. swiss cheese grated
- Dressing:
- 1/2 cup sugar
- 1/3 cup lemon juice
- 1/2 tsp. salt
- 1 1/2 T. Dijon mustard (use high-quality brand)
- 2/3 cup olive oil
- 1 T. poppy seed

Direction

- Place dressing ingredients into a container.
- Shake well to combine.
- Salad:
- Chop apple.
- Store in plastic bag with some lemon juice (additional amount from mentioned above-this helps keep the apple from turning brown)
- Measure the rest of the ingredients.
- DO NOT PUT TOGETHER UNTIL READY TO SERVE!

- Combine Salad ingredients.
- Drizzle dressing over and toss.
- Other variations include but are not limited to: strawberries, mandarin oranges, grapes, sunflower seeds, different kinds of cheeses, different kinds of dried fruit, left over chicken chopped etc.

185.   Apple Cranberry Salad Recipe

Serving: 8 | Prep: | Cook: | Ready in:

Ingredients

- 3 apples, red and green, cored and chopped
- into 1-inch pieces
- 1 cup celery, sliced on bias
- 3/4 cup sweetened-dried cranberries
- 1/2 cup hazelnuts, toasted and coarsley chopped
- 1/2 cup yogurt, plain, low fat
- 3 Tbsp orange juice concentrate, thawed
- 1/4 tsp salt

Direction

- Blend apples, celery, cranberries and hazelnuts in large bowl; set aside. Mix yogurt, orange juice concentrate and salt until blended. Pour over apple mixture and mix until blended. Makes 6-8 servings.

186.   Apple Crunch Salad Recipe

Serving: 8 | Prep: | Cook: 120mins | Ready in:

Ingredients

- 6 ounce package strawberry gelatin
- 2 cups boiling water

- 1-1/2 cups cold apple juice
- 1/2 teaspoon cinnamon
- 1 cup diced peeled apple
- 1/2 cup celery
- 1/4 cup chopped nuts

Direction

- Dissolve gelatin in boiling water.
- Add cold water and cinnamon.
- Chill until thickened.
- Gold in apple, celery and nuts.
- Spoon into 6 cup mold and chill until firm.

187.   Apple Feta Tossed Salad Recipe

Serving: 13 | Prep: | Cook: 15mins | Ready in:

Ingredients

- 1c walnut halves
- 5c torn romaine lettuce
- 5c torn red leaf lettuce
- 1/2c crumbled feta cheese
- 1/2c dried sweetened cranberries(craisins)
- 2 med. apples(your favorite variety)
- Dressing:
- 6Tbs olive oil
- 2Tbs white wine vinegar
- 2Tbs chopped onion
- 11/2tsp. dijon-style mustard
- 2 garlic cloves,minced(!/2 tsp minced)
- 1/2tsp sugar
- 1/4tsp dried basil
- 1/4tsp dried oregano
- 1/8tsp salt
- 1/8tsp dried parsley
- 1/8tsp black pepper

Direction

- In a large bowl, combine the salad ingredients, except for the apples. In a blender combine the dressing ingredients. Cover and process until well blended.

- Just prior to serving, peel and chop the apples and add to the salad.
- Drizzle the dressing over the salad and toss to coat. Serve.

188. Apple Madness Salad Recipe

Serving: 4 | Prep: | Cook: | Ready in:

Ingredients

- ½ onion
- 1 celery stalk
- cilantro
- 1 jalapeno pepper
- 2-3 tbsp apple cider vinegar
- 2 apples
- salt

Direction

- Just chop everything in the food processor and serve. That's it!

189. Apple Mallow Salad Recipe

Serving: 16 | Prep: | Cook: 10mins | Ready in:

Ingredients

- 1 can (20-oz.) crushed pineapple
- 1/2 cup sugar
- 1 Tbsp. all-purpose flour
- 1-2 Tbsp. white vinegar
- 1 egg, beaten
- 1 carton (12-oz.) frozen whipped topping, thawed
- 2 med. red apples, diced

- 2 med. green apples, diced
- 4 cups miniature marshmallows
- 1 cup honey roasted peanuts

Direction

- Drain pineapple, reserving juice; set pineapple aside.
- In a saucepan, combine sugar, flour, vinegar and reserved juice until smooth.
- Bring to a boil; cook and stir for 2 minutes or until thickened.
- Remove from heat.
- Stir in a small amount of hot mixture into egg; return all to pan, stirring constantly.
- Bring to a gentle boil; cook and stir for 2 minutes.
- Remove from the heat; cool.
- Fold whipped topping into the cooled mixture.
- Fold in apples, marshmallows and reserved pineapple.
- Cover and refrigerate for 1 hour.
- Just before serving, fold in peanuts.

190. Apple Salad Recipe

Serving: 8 | Prep: | Cook: | Ready in:

Ingredients

- 2 cups chopped apples
- 1 cup chopped celery
- 1 cup chopped walnuts
- 1 cup chopped water chestnuts
- 1 cup raisins
- 1 cup chopped pineapple
- 2/3 cup mayo
- 2 TBS brown sugar
- 1 TBS lemon juice

Direction

- Mix all the chopped ingredients together
- Mix the mayo, sugar and lemon juice together for dressing.

- Add the dressing to the salad and mix
- Add more dressing if salad is too dry
- Chill and Serve

191.   Apple Salad And Tofu Honey Cinnamon Dressing Recipe

Serving: 4 | Prep: | Cook: | Ready in:

Ingredients

- 2 granny smith apples sliced
- 2 gala apples sliced
- 1/4 cup fresh lemon juice
- 1 cup water
- 3 celery stalks sliced diagonally
- 8 ounces pineapple tidbits drained
- 1/3 cup walnuts coarsely chopped
- Fresh greens for serving
- Dressing:
- 1 cup plain yogurt
- 1/2 cup soft silken tofu
- 1 tablespoon honey
- 1 teaspoon ground cinnamon

Direction

- Place sliced apples in mixture of lemon juice and water.
- Add more water if needed to cover apples.
- At serving time drain liquid from apples.
- Combine apples, celery, pineapple and nuts.
- Combine yogurt, tofu, honey and cinnamon in a food processor and blend until smooth.
- Chill.
- Combine apple mixture with dressing and toss gently.
- Serve on a bed of fresh greens.

192.   Apple Salad For Diabetics Recipe

Serving: 8 | Prep: | Cook: | Ready in:

Ingredients

- 3 -1/2 cups apples unpeeled
- 1/3 cup chopped celery
- 1/4 cup raisins
- 1/4 cup chopped walnuts
- 1/2 cup plain yogurt
- 2 tablespoons sugar substitute
- 1/8 teaspoon ground cinnamon

Direction

- In bowl combine apples, celery, raisins and walnuts.
- In another bowl combine yogurt, sugar substitute and cinnamon until blended.
- Pour over apple mixture then toss to coat.
- Refrigerate until ready to serve.

193.   Apple Salad With Pecans Blue Cheese And Orange Vinaigrette Recipe

Serving: 4 | Prep: | Cook: 45mins | Ready in:

Ingredients

- 2 cups orange juice
- 2 tbls. balsamic vinegar
- 2 tbls. red onion, chopped
- 1 jalapeno pepper, seeded and chopped
- 3/4 cup olive oil
- 1 tbls. honey
- 1 tsp. kosher salt
- 1/2 tsp. ground pepper
- 2 granny smith apples, peeled, cored, cut into bite size pieces
- 1 head endive, washed, torn into pieces
- 1/2 cup pecan halves, toasted

- 1/2 cup blue cheese, crumbled

Direction

- Put orange juice in pan and bring to boil over high heat
- Reduce to 1/4 cup, about 30 minutes
- Let cool slightly
- In food processor, add orange reduction, Balsamic Vinegar, onion, and jalapeno and process until smooth
- With the motor running, slowly add olive oil until emulsified
- Add honey, salt and pepper, and pulse for just a second or 2
- Heat 3/4 cup of the orange vinaigrette in skillet over medium high heat
- Add apples and sauté, turning until just cooked through, 2-3 minutes
- Remove from skillet and cool to room temp.
- In mixing bowl, add endive and toss with 4 tbsp. orange vinaigrette
- Divide endive among 4 salad plates
- Put apples on top of endive
- Garnish with pecans and blue cheese
- Drizzle with remaining orange vinaigrette

194. Apple Sauerkraut Potato Salad Recipe

Serving: 4 | Prep: | Cook: 30mins | Ready in:

Ingredients

- 4 medium potatoes cut into 1/3" slices
- 1/3 cup cider vinegar
- 2 tablespoons vegetable oil
- 2 tablespoons water
- 1/4 teaspoon freshly ground black pepper
- 1 cup diced tart red apples
- 1 pound polish sausage sliced 1/3" thick
- 10 ounces sauerkraut rinsed and thoroughly drained
- 1/4 cup sliced green onions

- 1/4 cup chopped parsley
- 1/2 teaspoon salt

Direction

- In 2 quart saucepan over medium heat cook potatoes covered in 2" boiling water 12 minutes.
- Meanwhile in large bowl whisk together vinegar, oil, water and pepper then mix in apples.
- In large non-stick skillet over medium heat toss and brown sausage for 10 minutes.
- Remove with slotted spoon then drain on paper towels.
- Add potatoes, sauerkraut, onions, parsley and sausage to apple mixture then toss gently.
- Season with salt then serve immediately.

195. Apple Strawberry Spinach Salad Recipe

Serving: 4 | Prep: | Cook: | Ready in:

Ingredients

- 2 teaspoons salt
- 1/4 cup crumbled cooked bacon
- 1 small red onion grated
- 3/4 cup fresh bean sprouts
- 1/2 cup sliced fresh strawberries
- 2 cups chopped unpeeled granny smith apples
- 1 pound fresh spinach torn
- Dressing:
- 1/2 cup granulated sugar
- 2 teaspoons worcestershire sauce
- 1/3 cup white wine vinegar
- 3/4 cup vegetable oil

Direction

- In large salad bowl combine all salad ingredients and toss gently.
- Combine dressing ingredients and just before serving pour over salad and toss gently.

196. Apple Walnut And Fennel Salad Recipe

Serving: 4 | Prep: | Cook: | Ready in:

Ingredients

- 3 tablespoons olive oil
- 1 tablespoon sherry vinegar
- salt
- 2 ounces manchego cheese
- 1/2 fennel bulb
- 1 Granny Smith apple
- 1/3 cup chopped walnuts, toasted
- 1 tablespoon chopped chives
- 4 small fennel fronds for garnish

Direction

- 1. In a small bowl, whisk together the olive oil and sherry vinegar. Season with one-eighth teaspoon salt, or to taste. Reserve.
- 2. Cut the Manchego into batons about 2 inches long by one-fourth-inch thick. Slice the fennel lengthwise very thinly, preferably with a mandolin. Place the Manchego and fennel in a large bowl.
- 3. Core and halve the apple. Cut one-half of the apple into a one-fourth-inch dice. Thinly slice the second half lengthwise, preferably with a mandolin. Add the diced and sliced apple to the bowl, along with the walnuts.
- 4. Gently toss the salad, adding just enough vinaigrette to lightly coat the ingredients. Divide the salad among four plates. Evenly sprinkle the chives over each serving, and garnish each plate with one fennel frond. Serve immediately.

197. Apple Amp Potato Salad Recipe

Serving: 68 | Prep: | Cook: 15mins | Ready in:

Ingredients

- 8 Boiled and peeled potatoes, cut into thin slices
- 1/2 apple, finely diced
- 1/2 onion, finely diced
- 2 tb sweet relish
- 1 ts spicy mustard
- 2 tb pickle juice or 1/2 tsp vinegar and 1/2 tsp sugar
- 4 tb Heaping No Fat Miracle Whip
- paprika, salt & pepper -- to taste
- 4 Hard boiled eggs, diced

Direction

- Mix all ingredients together carefully, season to taste, garnish with parsley. Cool in refrigerator for at least 1-2 hrs. Best overnight.

198. Apple And Apricot Salad Recipe

Serving: 4 | Prep: | Cook: | Ready in:

Ingredients

- 2 large tart, crisp diced apples
- 1 tbls lemon juice
- ½ Cup diced dried apricots
- ½ Cup diced celery
- ¼ Cup chopped pecans
- 1/3 Cup active-culture vanilla yogurt

Direction

- Toss apples in lemon juice.
- Toss apples with other ingredients except for yogurt.
- Mix yogurt into salad and chill.

199. Apple And Banana Salad Recipe

Serving: 4 | Prep: | Cook: 5mins | Ready in:

Ingredients

- 1 egg separated
- 2/3 cup granulated
- 2 tablespoons flour
- 2 tablespoons butter
- 1 cup water
- 1 teaspoon vanilla

Direction

- Beat yolk of egg then add sugar, flour and butter then mix thoroughly.
- Put in saucepan and put on stove then add water and stir constantly until it boils.
- Let cool completely then add vanilla and gently fold in stiffly beaten egg white.
- Pour sauce over diced apples and bananas.

200. Apple And Beet Salad Recipe

Serving: 4 | Prep: | Cook: | Ready in:

Ingredients

- 1 large celery heart
- 2 medium beets cooked
- 1 large green apple
- 1 head endive
- 1 small head boston lettuce
- 3/4 cup walnut halves
- 2 scallions thinly sliced
- Basic Vinaigrette:
- 3/4 cup cold pressed olive oil
- 1/4 cup fresh lemon juice
- 1 teaspoon spicy mustard
- 2 cloves garlic
- 2 teaspoons fresh herbs
- 1/2 teaspoon salt
- 1/2 teaspoon freshly ground black pepper

Direction

- Cut celery heart, beets and apple into cubes.
- Wash greens and drain well then tear into bite size pieces.
- Combine all ingredients in a salad bowl.
- A few minutes before serving pour vinaigrette over salad and toss.
- To make vinaigrette combine olive oil, lemon juice and mustard in a jar with a lid.
- Crush or chop garlic finely then add garlic and herbs to oil mixture and shake well.
- Season with salt and pepper and shake again.

201. Apple And Green Chile Salad Recipe

Serving: 6 | Prep: | Cook: | Ready in:

Ingredients

- 2 cups chopped red and green apples
- 1 cup sliced celery
- 1/2 cup chopped walnuts toasted
- 1/2 cup diced green chilies
- 1/3 cup prepared ranch style salad dressing
- 1/4 cup mayonnaise
- lettuce leaves

Direction

- Combine apples, celery, nuts, chilies, salad dressing and mayonnaise in medium bowl.
- Cover then refrigerate 1 hour.
- Serve over lettuce.

202. Apple Bacon Salad Recipe

Serving: 8 | Prep: | Cook: 10mins | Ready in:

Ingredients

- 1/2 pound seedless red grapes
- 6 strips of bacon
- 1 large Granny Smith apple
- 1/2 celery stalk
- 1 cup shredded mix of Asiago, Romano, and parmesan cheeses (Kraft does a great combination of these)
- 1/2 cup plus 1tb apple cider vinegar
- 2tb olive oil
- 1 large bunch baby spinach
- 1 medium bunch watercress

Direction

- Fry up the bacon until browned.
- Meanwhile, pour 1/2 cup apple cider vinegar into medium-sized bowl.
- Halve the grape, dice the apple, and chop the celery.
- Put the above vegetables/fruits into the bowl of vinegar: swirl around so that all the surfaces get covered.
- Mix the watercress and spinach in a large salad bowl.
- Add the grapes, apple, and celery, being careful to siphon off the unused vinegar.
- Crumble the bacon on top.
- Add the 1 cup shredded cheeses.
- Whisk together the remaining 1tb apple cider vinegar and the 2tb olive oil. Add pepper and salt to taste (I recommend using a pepper grinder).
- Toss the salad with the dressing.
- Serve.

203. Apple Almond Kale Salad With Goat Cheese And Dried Cranberries Recipe

Serving: 4 | Prep: | Cook: 10mins | Ready in:

Ingredients

- i bunch Lacinato kale, rinsed, patted dry and chopped somewhat finely (1 " pieces) - about 3 or 4 cups
- 1/2 cup chopped sweet onion
- 1 Granny Smith apple, cored and sliced thin
- 1/2 cup dried cranberries
- 1/2 cup slivered almonds (toasted, if desired)
- 1 Tbsp lemon juice
- 3 oz. crumbled goat cheese (chèvre)
- Dressing:
- 1/4 cup balsamic dressing
- 1 clove garlic, grated or finely minced
- 1 tsp Dijon mustard
- 1 Tbsp shopped fresh herbs (basil, tarragon, oregano - whatever you prefer)
- 1 Tbsp maple syrup or honey
- 1/3 to 1/2 cup grape seed oil
- salt & pepper

Direction

- Combine kale, onion, apple, cranberries and almonds; sprinkle with lemon juice.
- Whisk together dressing ingredients and toss with vegetables; crumbled goat cheese on top and serve.

204. Apple Zucchini Salad Recipe

Serving: 4 | Prep: | Cook: | Ready in:

Ingredients

- 3 Tbsp. oil, preferably olive
- 1 1/2 tsp. lemon juice
- 1 Tbsp. cider vinegar

- 1/2 tsp. dried basil leaves, crumbled
- 1/4 tsp. salt
- 1/8 tsp. pepper
- 1/2 tsp. sugar
- 2 medium eating apples, cored and diced (I used gala apples)
- 1/2 medium red onion, cut lengthwise (store remainder in plastic in the refrigerator)
- 1 medium green pepper, chopped
- 1 medium zucchini, thinly sliced
- 2 stalks celery, thinly sliced

Direction

- To make dressing, blend in salad bowl the oil, lemon juice, vinegar basil, salt, pepper and sugar
- Add apples, onion, green pepper, celery and zucchini. Toss to coat.
- Cover Chill for 2 to 3 hours to blend flavors.

---

205. Apricot, Spinach And Bacon Salad Recipe

Serving: 4 | Prep: | Cook: |Ready in:

Ingredients

- Apricot, spinach and bacon Salad
- Indulge in a salad that is full of flavor and nutrition.
- From Hormel had to share it
- Rating: This recipe is recommended for 4 servings
- Ingredients1 (15-ounce) can black beans, drained and rinsed
- 1/2 cup chopped dried apricots
- 1/2 cup chopped bell pepper
- 2 tablespoons sliced green onions
- 1 tablespoon chopped fresh cilantro
- 1 clove garlic, minced
- 1/4 cup apricot nectar
- 2 tablespoons extra-virgin olive oil
- 2 tablespoons rice wine vinegar

Direction

- Apricot, Spinach and Bacon Salad (2 of 2) Ingredients (continued) 1 teaspoon House of Tsang® Ginger Flavored Soy Sauce
- 1 teaspoon grated peeled gingerroot
- 4 cups fresh spinach
- 1 cup Hormel® Real Crumbled Bacon
- Directions1.In large bowl, combine beans, apricots, bell pepper, onions, cilantro and garlic; mix well.
- 2. In jar with tight-fitting lid, combine apricot nectar, oil, vinegar, soy sauce and gingerroot; cover. Shake well.
- 3. Pour over bean mixture; toss to coat. Cover; refrigerate 2 to 24 hours.
- 4. Toss bean mixture with spinach and bacon to serve.
- © 2011 Hormel Foods Corporation

---

206. Arugula Fuji Apple Salad With Manchego Recipe

Serving: 4 | Prep: | Cook: |Ready in:

Ingredients

- 2 1/2 c. of Fresh baby arugula
- 2 fuji apples, cut into 1/4" Julienne (use Granny Smith's if you cannot find fuji apples)
- 1/2 c. dried cherries or dried cranberries
- 1/4 lb. Manchego or Similar nutty cheese
- juice of one lemon
- *4 Tbsp. truffle oil (Use a very high quality EVOO if you don't have or can't find truffle oil)
- 1 tsp. kosher salt
- fresh cracked pepper to taste

Direction

- Combine Arugula, Apples, and Cherries into a cold mixing bowl.
- Sprinkle the salt, lemon juice, truffle oil and lightly toss.

- Even distribute onto salad plates.
- Using a vegetable peeler, shave the Manchego cheese over the salad.
- Serve with fresh cracked pepper.

207. Arugula/tango/oak/sweet Gem Lettuce Salad With Grapefruit With A Lemon Honey Dressing Recipe

Serving: 4 | Prep: | Cook: 15mins | Ready in:

Ingredients

- 3 cups of the assorted lettuces
- 1 grapefruit peeled, sectioned and chopped
- 2 tablespoons chopped fresh cilantro
- lemon honey Dressing
- 1 tablespoon lemon juice
- 1 tablespoon honey

Direction

- Mix the first three ingredients together in a bowl and then whisk the lemon juice and honey in another bowl and then pour the dressing over the salad

208. Asian Inspired Mango Slaw Recipe

Serving: 4 | Prep: | Cook: 10mins | Ready in:

Ingredients

- 2 small mangoes or 1 large one, cut into 'slivered' pieces (see instructions)
- 3 tbsp sugar
- 3 tbsp seasoned rice vinegar
- 1-2 jalapeños, cut into very thin slivers
- 2 tbsp chopped cilantro

- 10 - 16 ounces of shredded cabbage mix (pre-bagged works perfectly)
- 1/2 red bell pepper, cut into slivered matchsticks
- 1 carrot, cut into slivered matchsticks

Direction

- PREPARE THIS JUST BEFORE SERVING FOR BEST RESULTS! Cut the mango into 'slivered' pieces to mimic the shape of your shredded cabbage. Meanwhile, stir sugar and vinegar in small heat proof measuring cup and microwave until sugar dissolves (try 30 sec and stir; repeat in 10 sec increments until sugar is dissolved into the vinegar.)
- Place mangoes, jalapeño, cabbage, cilantro, green onions, bell pepper and carrots in medium bowl. Pour cooled vinegar dressing mixture over and toss to coat. Season with salt and pepper.
- Let the slaw sit and marinate while grilling or preparing fish or chicken.

209. Asparagus Apple And Chicken Salad Recipe

Serving: 8 | Prep: | Cook: | Ready in:

Ingredients

- 1 cup fresh asparagus cut in 1 inch pieces
- 2 tablespoons cider vinegar
- 2 tablespoons vegetable oil
- 2 teaspoons honey
- 2 teaspoons minced fresh parsley
- 1/2 teaspoon salt
- 1/4 teaspoons pepper
- 1 cup cubed cooked chicken
- 1/2 cup diced red apple
- 2 cups torn mixed greens

Direction

- Cook asparagus in a small amount of water until tender crisp.
- Drain and cool.
- In a bowl combine the next six ingredients.
- Stir in chicken, apple and asparagus and toss.
- Serve over greens.

210. Autumn Apple Salad Recipe

Serving: 8 | Prep: | Cook: 5mins | Ready in:

Ingredients

- 1 large can crushed pineapple drained
- 2/3 cup sugar
- 1 package lemon gelatin
- 8 ounce package cream cheese softened
- 1 cup diced apples
- 1/2 cup chopped pecans
- 1 cup chopped celery
- 1 cup Cool Whip

Direction

- Combine pineapple and sugar in a sauce pan then bring to a boil for 3 minutes.
- Add gelatin and stir until dissolved then add cream cheese stirring until smooth.
- Cool then fold in apples, pecans, celery and cool whip.
- Pour into a rectangular dish and refrigerate.

211. Autumn Apple Salad With Creamy Maple Dressing Recipe

Serving: 4 | Prep: | Cook: 25mins | Ready in:

Ingredients

- Dressing:
- 1/2 c canola oil

- 1/4 c maple syrup
- 1/4 c mayonnaise
- 3 Tbs white wine vinegar
- 2 tsp sugar
- salt and pepper to taste
- Salad:
- 1 bag(5 oz) mixed baby greens
- 2 Gala or red delicious apples,cored and chopped
- 1/2 c dried cranberries
- 1/2 c chopped walnuts,toasted

Direction

- Whisk together syrup, mayonnaise, vinegar and sugar in medium bowl. Whisk oil in gradually until mixture thickens slightly. Season to taste with salt and pepper.
- Toss together greens, apples, cranberries and half the walnuts in a large bowl. Toss with enough dressing to coat.
- Divide salad equally among plates. Sprinkle with remaining walnuts. Serve

212. Autumn Salad With Grapes, Walnuts And Parmesan Recipe

Serving: 8 | Prep: | Cook: 25mins | Ready in:

Ingredients

- 1/2 pound seedless red or purple grapes
- 1 tablespoon minced shallot
- 1 tablespoon (or more) Sherry vinegar
- 1/4 teaspoon kosher salt plus more for seasoning
- 1/4 cup extra-virgin olive oil
- 1 tablespoon apple balsamic vinegar plus more for drizzling
- Freshly ground black pepper
- 1/2 pound greens (butter lettuce, endive and radicchio) (about 8 cups)

- 1/4 pound Roncal, Manchego, or pecorino cheese, shaved with a peeler
- 3/4 cup roasted walnuts, coarsely chopped

Direction

- Finely chop 7 grapes; transfer to a small bowl. Cut remaining grapes in half; transfer to another small bowl and set aside. Using a fork, mash chopped grapes in bowl into a purée. Stir in shallot, 1 tablespoon Sherry vinegar, and 1/4 teaspoon salt and let sit for 5 minutes. Whisk in oil and 1 tablespoon balsamico. Season vinaigrette to taste with salt, pepper, and more Sherry vinegar, if desired. DO AHEAD: Vinaigrette and halved grapes can be prepared 8 hours ahead. Cover and chill vinaigrette and grapes separately. Bring vinaigrette to room temperature and re-whisk before continuing.
- Combine greens and halved grapes in a large bowl; drizzle with vinaigrette and season with salt and pepper. Toss salad to coat. Arrange salad on chilled dinner plates, dividing evenly. Scatter cheese and walnuts over. Drizzle salads with more apple balsamico.

---

213. Avacado And Blueberry Salad Recipe

Serving: 6 | Prep: | Cook: 15mins | Ready in:

Ingredients

- 2 tbsp. honey
- 1/4 cup plain non-fat yogurt
- 1/2 tsp. ground cinnamon
- 1/4 cup fresh orange or grapefruit juice
- 1/8 tsp. salt
- 1 ripe, fresh avacado,peeled, seeded, cut into slices
- 1 cup fresh blueberries, rinsed, picked over, well drained
- 2 medium sliced apples, peeled,cored,seeded, diced

- 2 cups fresh mango chunks
- 1 (5oz.) package mixed baby greens
- 2 tbsp. chives or green onions, chopped
- 2 tsp. walnuts, toasted, chopped coarsley

Direction

- In a medium bowl, mix honey, yogurt and cinnamon together until smooth and creamy. Whisk in juice; stir in salt and pepper. Taste and adjust seasoning.
- Place chopped avocado, blueberries, apple, and mango in medium bowl and toss with about 2/3 of the tangy dressing; set aside.
- Toss salad greens in large bowl with remainder of tangy dressing, and distribute evenly on each of six salad plates. Place an equal portion of dressed fruit/avocado mixture on top of each greens serving. Sprinkle with chopped chives and toasted walnuts to serve.
- *To toast walnuts, place nut pieces in dry skillet over medium-high heat and stir occasionally for about seven minutes, or until pieces are browned lightly. Remove from heat. Let nuts cool slightly before chopping and using to garnish salad.
- Nutrition Facts:

---

214. Avocado Mango Broccoli Salad Recipe

Serving: 4 | Prep: | Cook: 30mins | Ready in:

Ingredients

- 2 ripe avocados
- 2 ripe mangoes
- 2-3 cups broccoli, chopped
- 1/2 cup red onion, chopped
- 1/2 cup craisins
- Himalayan salt and pepper, to taste

Direction

- Combine all ingredients. Chill and serve.

215. Avocado Mango Salad Recipe

Serving: 0 | Prep: | Cook: 30mins | Ready in:

Ingredients

- •½ cup finely chopped parsley
- •¼ cup peanut or canola oil
- •¼ cup lime juice
- •2 tbsp orange juice
- •1 jalapeño, stemmed, seeded, and minced
- •salt and pepper to taste
- •2 ripe mangoes, peeled, pitted, and cut into ¼-inch cubes
- •2 ripe avocados, pitted, peeled, and cut into 1-inch chunks
- •1 small navel orange, peeled and cut into segments
- •2 tsp unsweetened shredded coconut (optional)

Direction

- • Whisk together 6 tbsp. parsley, oil, both citrus juices, jalapeño, and salt and pepper in a large bowl.
- • Add mango and avocado and toss gently to combine;
- • Cover with plastic wrap and refrigerate to meld flavors, about 1 hour.
- • To serve, transfer chilled avocado salad to a serving bowl;
- • Halve orange segments crosswise and lay over salad.
- • Sprinkle with remaining parsley, and coconut if using.

216. BEET N APPLE AUTUMN SALAD Recipe

Serving: 4 | Prep: | Cook: 10mins | Ready in:

Ingredients

- Dressing:
- 1/4 cup olive oil
- 2 tbsp lime juice
- 1 tbsp lime zest
- 1 tbsp dill
- 1 tbsp Dijon mustard
- 1/4 tsp salt
- 1/8 tsp pepper
- Salad:
- 1 small head of romaine lettuce
- 1 GRANNY SMITH apple
- 1/2 lb cooked beets or 1-14oz can of beets drained

Direction

- Wisk all DRESSING ingredients together.
- Chill.
- Meanwhile tear the lettuce into bite size pieces and place in a large bowl.
- Toss with half of the dressing.
- Dice the apple and scatter over the lettuce. Peel beets, dice and top lettuce & apples. Pour remaining dressing and toss.

217. Banana Grape Waldorf Salad With Lime Cream Recipe

Serving: 0 | Prep: | Cook: 15mins | Ready in:

Ingredients

- 1/4 cup mayonnaise (I like the added "zing" of Miracle Whip)
- 1/4 cup sour cream or yogurt
- 1 tsp lime juice, divided
- 1 tart apple, diced (unpeeled for extra color)
- 1 banana, peeled and sliced

- 1/2 cup red grapes, halved
- 1/4 cup dried cranberries
- toasted almonds, peanuts, cashews, etc. for garnish

Direction

- Combine mayo or Miracle Whip with sour cream/yogurt and 1/2 tsp. lime juice.
- Cut fruit and toss with additional lime juice to prevent browning. Fold in dressing and dried cranberries.
- Chill at least one hour before serving (if possible).
- Serve the salad piled on a lettuce leaf. Garnish with toasted almonds, peanuts, or cashew pieces.

218.   Banana Nut Salad Recipe

Serving: 0 | Prep: | Cook: 30mins | Ready in:

Ingredients

- 1 tablespoon creamy peanut butter
- 1 tablespoon honey
- 1/4 cup mayonnaise or salad dressing
- 3 bananas
- lemon juice
- Bibb or Romaine leaves
- 1/2 cup chopped peanuts

Direction

- In a small bowl, stir together the peanut butter and honey. Blend in mayonnaise or salad dressing.
- Slice bananas diagonally into 1/2" slices; dip in lemon juice. Arrange banana slices on lettuce leaves on salad plates. Drizzle peanut butter mixture over bananas; sprinkle with nuts.

219.   Beet And Apple Salad Recipe

Serving: 6 | Prep: | Cook: 2mins | Ready in:

Ingredients

- 2 Tbl. honey
- 2 Tbl. apple cider vinegar
- 2 Tbl. olive oil
- 2 cans sliced beets (I use the ones in a jar)
- 1 fuji apple
- 1/4 C crumbled blue cheese
- 1-2 tsp chopped parsley
- salt and pepper to taste (optional)

Direction

- Make dressing:
- Whisk together honey, vinegar, and olive oil. Season with salt and pepper to taste. Set aside.
- Rinse and drain beets.
- Cut apple into slices.
- Gently toss beet and apple slices with dressing, coating well.
- Top with blue cheese and parsley.

220.   Belgian Endive Apple And Almond Salad Recipe

Serving: 4 | Prep: | Cook: | Ready in:

Ingredients

- 2 single tart green apples peeled and cut into 1/2" cubes
- 3 single Belgian endives thinly sliced crosswise
- 2 tablespoon almonds peeled and shelled
- Dressing:
- 4 teaspoons oil
- 1 tablespoon lemon juice
- 1 teaspoon minced garlic
- 1/4 teaspoon salt

Direction

- Mix apple, endives and almonds together in a bowl.
- Mix dressing and pour on salad then toss thoroughly and serve.

221. Berry Spinach Salad Recipe

Serving: 0 | Prep: | Cook: 20mins | Ready in:

Ingredients

- 1 bag baby spinach
- 1 pint fresh strawberries, sliced
- 1 pint fresh blueberries
- 1/4 c. red onion, sliced in half-rings
- 1/4 c. cilantro, chopped
- 1/2 c. feta or bleu cheese, crumbled
- 1 c. pecans, caramelized with sugar on the stove
- watermelon or berry vinaigrette

Direction

- Combine all ingredients. Chill until ready to serve. Toss with vinaigrette.

222. Black Rice Salad With Kiwifruit & Cashews Recipe

Serving: 6 | Prep: | Cook: 15mins | Ready in:

Ingredients

- 2 tbsp lemon juice
- 2 tbsp olive oil
- 2 tsp honey
- 1 tsp Dijon mustard
- 1/2 tsp salt
- 1/4 tsp pepper
- 1 clove garlic, finely chopped

- 2 1/2 cups cooked and cooled black or brown rice
- 2 Zespri SunGold kiwifruit, peeled and cut up
- 1 cup quartered strawberries
- 1/4 cup red onion, chopped
- 2 tsp fresh mint, chopped
- 1/3 cup salted cashew pieces

Direction

- In small bowl, whisk together lemon juice, olive oil, honey, mustard, garlic, salt and pepper.
- In large bowl, stir dressing into rice. Stir in remaining ingredients except cashews. Cover and refrigerate up to 2 hours before serving to allow flavours to blend. Stir in cashews just before serving. Tip: A serrated peeler works best for peeling kiwifruit.

223. Broccoli Apple Salad Recipe

Serving: 12 | Prep: | Cook: 3mins | Ready in:

Ingredients

- 5 cups broccoli, chopped
- 1 red onion, chopped
- 2 cups crisp red apples, chopped
- 10 strips bacon, fried and crumbled or use real bacon bits
- 1 cup sunflower seeds
- 1 cup white raisins
- 1 cup craisins
- Grated carrot for color
- Dressing:
- 1 cup mayonaise
- 3 tbsp. sour cream
- 3 tbsp sugar
- 3 tbsp. vinegar.

Direction

- Mix all the ingredients together in a large bowl.
- Mix dressing ingredients together in a medium size bowl.
- Pour dressing over broccoli mixture.
- Refrigerate until chilled and enjoy!

224. Broccoli Salad Recipe

Serving: 6 | Prep: | Cook: |Ready in:

Ingredients

- 1 or more broccoli heads, cut into tiny florets
- 1/2 to 1 cup raisins
- 1/2 cup red onion, finely chopped
- 1/2 cup celery (optional)
- 1/2 to 1 cup sunflower seeds
- 5 to 10 slices bacon , cut into 1 inch pieces for frying crisp.
- DRESSING
- 3/4 cup to 1 cup mayonnaise
- 1/4 to 1/2 cup sugar
- 3 T red wine vinegar

Direction

- Steam or blanch or zap broccoli florets in microwave, a minute at a time, checking for "bright green". Set aside to cool
- Throw the raisins, chopped red onion, and celery into large bowl.
- Cook the bacon, either in a skillet on the stove, or zap between paper towels. Check the cooking after 2 minutes for 4 slices, 3 minutes for 5 slices. Get as crisp as possible without burning. Drain on clean paper towels. When cool, crumble the bacon.
- Now make the dressing by combining the dressing ingredients. Add the cooled florets of broccoli to the big bowl, toss the ingredients a bit to combine and add the dressing. Then just before serving, add the sunflower seeds and crumbled bacon. Toss again. Enjoy!!

225. Broccoli, Cauliflower And Bacon Salad Recipe

Serving: 8 | Prep: | Cook: 30mins |Ready in:

Ingredients

- 4 cups broccoli florets
- 4 cups cauliflower florets
- 1 cup dried cranberries
- 2 "red" apples, diced (I used fuji apples)
- 2 granny smith apples, diced
- 3 green onions, thinly sliced
- 1 pound maple flavored bacon, cooked crisp and crumbled
- 4 tablespoons lemon juice, divided
- 1 cup mayonnaise (can use "light" mayo if desired)
- 3 tablespoons maple syrup

Direction

- Blanch broccoli and cauliflower in boiling salted water for 2 minutes. Plunge into a boil of ice water to stop cooking process. (You can skip this step if you want, but I find it takes some of the bitterness out of the vegetables.)
- Drain vegetables and place in large bowl. Add 1 tablespoon lemon juice to diced apple to prevent browning. Add apples, cranberries, green onion and bacon and toss to combine.
- Combine mayonnaise, remaining 3 tablespoons lemon juice and maple syrup until smooth. Pour over salad.
- Gently stir. Cover and chill at least one hour.

226. CARAMEL APPLE SALAD Recipe

Serving: 8 | Prep: | Cook: |Ready in:

Ingredients

- 1 small container Cool Whip
- 1 pkg. dry instant butterscotch pudding
- 1 (8-oz) can crushed pineapple with juice
- 3 C. diced apples
- 1 C mini marshmallows

Direction

- Mix cool whip, butterscotch pudding and crushed pineapple with juice.
- Add apples and marshmallows.
- Keep in refrigerator until ready to serve.

227. CARROT APPLE SALAD Recipe

Serving: 6 | Prep: | Cook: 180mins | Ready in:

Ingredients

- Ingredients:
- 1 can (8-oz) unsweetened crushed pineapple
- 2 medium tart apples, diced
- 3 cups shredded carrots
- 3 Tbs. raisins
- 3 Tbs. flaked coconut
- 1/3 cup fat-free reduced-sugar vanilla yogurt
- 1/3 cup fat-free plain yogurt
- 3 Tbs. reduced-fat mayonnaise or salad dressing
- 1 Tbs. lemon juice

Direction

- Drain pineapple, reserving juice in a bowl. Add apples to the juice; toss to coat. Let stand for 5 minutes; drain. In a large bowl, combine the pineapple, carrots, raisins, coconut and apples. In a small bowl, combine the remaining ingredients. Pour over carrot mixture and toss to coat. Cover and refrigerate for 3 – 4 hours or until chilled.
- Serving size: ¾ cup
- Calories per serving: 138, Fat: 4g, Cholesterol: 3mg, Sodium: 101mg, Carbohydrate: 26g

- Diabetic Friendly
- Diabetic Exchanges: 1 fruit, 1 veg, ½ starch, ½ fat

228. CRUNCHY APPLE SALAD Recipe

Serving: 8 | Prep: | Cook: | Ready in:

Ingredients

- 1 small pkg. package strawberry jello
- 2 C. boiling water
- 1-1/2 C. cold apple juice
- 1/4 tsp. cinnamon
- 1 C. peeled and diced golden delicious apple
- 1/4 C. chopped walnuts

Direction

- Dissolve Jell-O in boiling water.
- Add cold water and cinnamon.
- Chill until thickened.
- Fold in apple and walnuts.
- Spoon into mold and chill until firm.

229. Cabbage And Apple Salad Recipe

Serving: 6 | Prep: | Cook: | Ready in:

Ingredients

- 2 cups shredded cabbage
- 1 cup tart apples cut into strips
- 1/4 cup mayonnaise
- 1/2 teaspoon salt
- 1 tablespoon freshly lemon juice
- 1 teaspoon sugar

Direction

- Combine cabbage with apples then add mayonnaise, salt, lemon juice and sugar.
- Toss well to combine then chill at least 1 hour before serving.

---

230. Cabbage And Apple Salad Recipe

Serving: 4 | Prep: | Cook: | Ready in:

Ingredients

- 2-3 cups red cabbage, shredded
- 1 medium apple, unpeeled and diced
- 1 tablespoon lemon juice
- 1/2 cup raisins, I like golden raisins
- 1/4 cup pineapple juice
- 1-1/2 teaspoons lemon juice
- 1/4 teaspoon salt
- 1 tablespoon granulated sugar
- 3/4 - 1 cup sour cream

Direction

- Prepare cabbage and apple.
- Use 1 Tbsp. lemon juice to wet diced apple to prevent darkening.
- Toss shredded cabbage, raisins, and apple.
- Mix fruit juices, salt, and sugar.
- Add sour cream, stir until smooth and add to the salad.
- Chill for at least 1 hour before serving.

---

231. Cantaloupe And Tomato Salad Recipe

Serving: 6 | Prep: | Cook: 10mins | Ready in:

Ingredients

- 1 med ripe cantaloupe seeded and cubed or melon balled

- 1 to 2 cup halved cherry tomatoes
- 1 /4 cup chopped fresh basil
- 1 to 2 tbs fresh minced red onion
- 2 tbs lemon juice -fresh
- 2 Tbs fresh orange juice
- 1 tsp fresh grated orange rind

Direction

- Simple mix all gently
- May serve immediately or chilled

---

232. Cantaloupe Cucumber Juice Recipe

Serving: 2 | Prep: | Cook: 15mins | Ready in:

Ingredients

- 1 cucumber
- 1 cup cantaloupe
- 1.5 inch square piece of ginger, with peel removed
- 1 gala apple
- 1 kiwi
- 1 half cup pineapple chunks, fresh

Direction

- Cut all produce small enough to feed through juicer and push through juicer by alternating hard fruits with the softer ones. Serve with a couple of ice cubes if desired.

---

233. Cantaloupe/honeydew With Lime & Cilantro Recipe

Serving: 4 | Prep: | Cook: 15mins | Ready in:

Ingredients

- 1/2 cantaloupe, seeded, peeled and cut into bite size pieces

- 1/2 honeydew, seeded, peeled and cut into bite size pieces
- 1 lime juiced
- 1 1/2 tablespoons roughly chopped cilantro
- salt to taste

Direction

- Place all ingredients into bowl and toss

234. Caramel Apple Salad Recipe

Serving: 6 | Prep: | Cook: 10mins | Ready in:

Ingredients

- 1 tablespoon flour
- 1/3 cup sugar
- 1 egg
- 2 tablespoons apple cider vinegar
- 1 can (8oz. size)crushed pineapple - drained, but reserve juice
- 4 red delicious apples (or granny smith) unpeeled, cored and chopped. (use both if ya want)
- 1 cup salted peanuts
- 1 container (8z. size) Cool-whip or store brand

Direction

- Mix flour & sugar
- Beat in egg and add to the flour & sugar. Mix well
- Add vinegar and pineapple juice.
- Cook in small pan over low heat stirring until thick.
- Cool completely
- Meanwhile, combine apples, pineapple & peanuts.
- Pour cooled dressing over all.
- Fold in cool-whip.
- Chill well and enjoy!

235. Carrot Apple Rasin Salad Recipe

Serving: 2 | Prep: | Cook: | Ready in:

Ingredients

- Ingredients:
- 3 carrots
- 1/2 apple
- 3/8 cups natural yogurt
- 1/4 cup chopped celery
- 1 tablespoon chopped parsley
- 1 tablespoon lemon juice
- 1/2 tablespoon honey
- salt and pepper to taste
- raisins for sweetness if you wish

Direction

- Directions:
- Peel and grate the carrots and apple.
- Place the mixture in a dish before, add the celery and parsley.
- Mix the yogurt, honey and lemon.
- Add salt, pepper and pour over salad.

236. Carrot Raisin Salad Recipe

Serving: 2 | Prep: | Cook: 20mins | Ready in:

Ingredients

- 4-5 carrots, shredded
- 1 T honey
- 1/4 c mayo
- small box of golden raisins

Direction

- Combine and chill.

237. Carrot And Apple Salad Recipe

Serving: 4 | Prep: | Cook: |Ready in:

Ingredients

- 1 lb carrots
- 3 apples, peeled
- 3 tablespoons extra virgin olive oil
- 1/2 lemon
- 1 tablespoon orange flower water
- salt
- pepper

Direction

- Finely grate carrots and apples and place in a salad bowl.
- Make dressing with olive oil, the juice from half a lemon, and stir in the orange-flower water.
- Season with salt and pepper and pour over salad and toss lightly.
- Chill thoroughly and serve.

238. Champagne Mango, Avocado, & Tomato Salad Recipe

Serving: 2 | Prep: | Cook: 5mins |Ready in:

Ingredients

- 1 champagne mango, peeled and cubed
- 1 ripe avocado, peeled and cubed
- 1 vine tomato, diced
- 2 green onions, trimmed & chopped
- several handfuls of baby romaine or other baby greens
- 2 tbsp olive oil
- 1 tbsp orange Muscat champagne vinegar (from Trader Joe's, or similar)

- black pepper to taste, freshly ground

Direction

- Mix oil, vinegar, and pepper well. Combine dressing with other ingredients & toss gently to coat.

239. Chavrie Goat Cheese Fennel Apple Salad Recipe

Serving: 4 | Prep: | Cook: |Ready in:

Ingredients

- 1 pkg. (5.3 oz) Chavrie® goat cheese
- 2 ea. gala apples
- 1 ea. celery stalk
- 1 ea. fennel bulb
- ½ tsp. lemon juice
- ½ C walnut pieces

Direction

- Remove core and slice apples.
- Remove core and slice fennel.
- Cross cut celery.
- Mix apples, fennel and celery with lemon juice in a stainless steel bowl.
- Fold in Chavrie®.
- Serve on a bed of baby salad and top with walnut pieces

240. Cherry Arugula Salad Recipe

Serving: 6 | Prep: | Cook: 10mins |Ready in:

Ingredients

- 2 1/2 tablespoons balsamic vinegar
- 1 small shallot, chopped
- 1 1/2 teaspoons Dijon mustard

- 1 tablespoon water
- 6 tablespoons slivered almonds, divided
- 1/2 pound cherries (about 2 cups), pitted and halved, divided
- 2 tablespoons chopped fresh tarragon
- 5 ounces baby arugula
- 1 1/2 cups cooked whole grains (e.g. barley, farro, wheat berries, wild rice)

Direction

- In a blender, combine vinegar, shallot, mustard, water, 3 tablespoons of the almonds and 1/4 cup of the pitted cherries. Blend until very smooth, about 1 minute. Stir in tarragon.
- Combine arugula, cooked grains and remaining cherries in a large bowl. Toss with the dressing and garnish with the remaining 3 tablespoons almonds.

---

241. Cherry And Apple Chicken Salad Recipe

Serving: 6 | Prep: | Cook: |Ready in:

Ingredients

- 3 cooked boneless chicken breast halves diced
- 1/3 cup dried cherries
- 1/3 cup diced celery
- 1/3 cup toasted chopped pecans
- 1/3 cup mayonnaise
- 1 tablespoon buttermilk
- 1/2 teaspoon salt
- 1/2 teaspoon freshly ground black pepper
- 1/3 cup cubed apples

Direction

- In large bowl combine chicken, cherries, celery, nuts, mayonnaise, milk, salt, pepper and apple.
- Toss together well and refrigerate until chilled.
- Serve on toasted bread of choice or croissants.

---

242. Chicken And Spring Mix Salad With Spicy Pineapple Dressing Recipe

Serving: 2 | Prep: | Cook: 30mins |Ready in:

Ingredients

- •1/2 lb skinless, boneless chicken breast
- •1 tsp paprika (or chili powder) •1/2 tsp salt
- •1/2 tsp garlic powder
- •1 cup cubed fresh pineapple (about 8 ounces), divided
- •1 tbsp orange juice (or apple juice)
- •2 tbsp apple cider vinegar (or vinegar + 1 tsp sugar)•1/2 serrano pepper, seeded (or habanero)
- •1 tbsp olive oil (extra-virgin if available)•1/3 red bell pepper, thinly sliced•1/4 red onion, thinly sliced•1 (5-ounce) package fresh spring mix of spinach, baby lettuce, and radicchio

Direction

- 1. Heat a non-stick pan over medium-high heat with 1 tbsp. olive oil. Sprinkle both sides of chicken evenly with paprika, garlic powder, and salt. Add chicken to pan; cook for 5 minutes on each side or until well browned. Remove from pan; set aside.
- 2. Combine half of pineapple, orange juice, vinegar, and Serrano in a blender; process until smooth. Add olive oil after blended and mix with spoon or ladle.
- 3. Cut the red onion and red bell pepper into thin strips or desired pieces. Pineapples should be cut into 1/2-inch chunks or can be cut according to preference as well.
- 4. Combine remaining pineapple and the remaining ingredients in a large bowl. Drizzle with 3/4 cup dressing, and toss gently to coat. Divide salad evenly among 2 plates. Cut chicken across the grain into thin slices; divide chicken evenly over salads. Drizzle salad evenly with remaining dressing. Enjoy!

243. Chicken Apple Salad With Blue Cheese Dressing Recipe

Serving: 8 | Prep: | Cook: 10mins | Ready in:

Ingredients

- 8 slices bacon
- 1 cup chopped pecans
- 4 cups torn romaine, arugula and/or spinach
- 1 cup finely chopped apple
- 2-1/2 cups shredded or cubed rotisserie chicken
- 1/2 small red onion thinly sliced
- 2 tablespoons crumbled blue cheese
- Dressing:
- 2 cups buttermilk
- 1 cup crumbled blue cheese
- 1 cup diary sour cream
- 1/4 cup mayonnaise
- 1/4 cup Dijon mustard
- 1 tablespoon lemon juice
- 3 cloves garlic chopped
- 1 teaspoon freshly ground black pepper

Direction

- Cook bacon in a skillet over medium heat.
- Drain on paper towels reserving 2 tablespoons drippings in skillet.
- Add pecans to skillet and sauté until toasted.
- In large bowl toss greens with pecans, crumbled bacon and apple.
- Divide among four dinner plates and arrange chicken slices on top of each salad.
- Top each salad with onion and blue cheese.
- Serve with dressing.
- To make dressing combine all ingredients in blender and process until smooth.

244. Chicken Pecan Apple Salad My Way Recipe

Serving: 4 | Prep: | Cook: 20mins | Ready in:

Ingredients

- For the Sauce
- 1 T dry mustard
- 1 t water
- 1 t white wine or apple cider vinegar
- 2 T mayonaise (I have used Miracle Whip too in a pinch)
- pinch sugar
- 1 T honey
- 1 small clove garlic, grated
- 1/2 t horseradish sauce
- 1 T Tiger sauce (optional but awesome)
- Everything else
- 4 c (approx.) chicken
- 1 stalk celery, diced
- 1 c apple - diced
- 2 T mayo
- 1/4 c dried currants or cherries (optional)
- 1/2 c toasted pecans
- salt and pepper to taste

Direction

- Mix ingredients for sauce - set aside
- Mix sauce, chicken, fruit and celery in bowl....if you salad needs to be wetter, gradually add from the 2 T of mayo until it suits you (I usually don't need to add the additional mayo)
- Salt and pepper to taste
- EAT

245. Chicken Salad With Grapes And Homemade Mayo Recipe

Serving: 0 | Prep: | Cook: 25mins | Ready in:

Ingredients

- For the homemade mayo:
- 1 egg yolk
- 1 tsp. vinegar (coconut is perfect but can use white wine or apple cider)
- 1/2 Tbs. mustard (I use dijon)
- 1 cup avocado oil OR extra light olive oil
- S&P
- For the chicken salad:
- 2 1/2 cups chopped cooked chicken
- 1/2-1 cup grapes, halved
- 3 carrots, grated
- 1 jalapeno, chopped (can be omitted)
- 1 roasted pepper, chopped
- 1 tomato, chopped
- Handful cilantro, chopped
- 1 tsp. garlic powder
- 1 tsp. onion powder
- 1/2 tsp. paprika (smoked is really good in this)

Direction

- Start with the mayo. Add the egg yolk first into a medium size bowl (need a lot of room to whisk!) Next add in the vinegar, mustard and a little bit of salt and pepper. Whisk until well combined. SLOWLY start adding oil while vigorously whisking the whole time. This will take a good 5-10 mins. And yes it is a good arm workout :) If you add the oil too fast it will break and not be usable. Taste when done and add more salt if needed.
- For the chicken salad just add everything into a bowl, including all of the mayo you just made and stir . Serve on bread or a croissant, in a pita, or over a salad like I did this time :)

---

246.   Chicken Waldorf Salad Recipe

Serving: 4 | Prep: | Cook: | Ready in:

Ingredients

- 2/3 cup mayonnaise
- 2 tablespoons lemon juice
- 1/2 teaspoon salt
- 1/4 teaspoon ground pepper
- 2 cup cooked chicken, diced
- 2 red apples, cored and diced
- 2/3 cup celery, sliced
- 1/2 cup chopped walnuts

Direction

- Combine mayonnaise, lemon juice, salt and pepper in a bowl.
- Add the chicken, apples and celery.
- Toss to coat.
- Cover and chill.
- Toss with walnuts just before serving.

---

247.   Chopped Apple Salad With Toasted Walnuts Goat Cheese And Pomegranate Vinaigrette Recipe

Serving: 8 | Prep: | Cook: | Ready in:

Ingredients

- pomegranate Vinaigrette:
- 1/4 cup pomegranate molasses
- 2 tablespoons red wine vinegar
- 1 heaping tablespoon Dijon mustard
- 1 tablespoon honey, or more to taste
- salt
- Freshly ground black pepper
- 3/4 cup extra-virgin olive oil
- Salad:
- 6 apples (Granny Smith, Gala, Fuji) any or a combination of all, skin left on, core removed and cut into 1/2-inch dice
- 2 cups baby spinach
- 2 cups of baby romaine
- 1 cup toasted coarsely chopped walnuts
- 3/4 pound crumbled goat cheese (chevre)
- salt

- Freshly ground black pepper

Direction

- Whisk together the pomegranate molasses, vinegar, mustard, honey and salt and pepper in a medium bowl. Slowly whisk in the olive oil until emulsified.
- For the salad:
- Combine the apples, spinach, endive, walnuts and blue cheese in a large bowl. Add the vinaigrette and toss to coat, season with salt and pepper, to taste

248. Chunky Cinnamon & Sugar Applesauce Recipe

Serving: 6 | Prep: | Cook: 45mins | Ready in:

Ingredients

- 8 cups chopped, peeled tart cooking apples
- 1/2 cup packed brown sugar
- 2 teaspoons vanilla extract
- 1 teaspoon ground cinnamon

Direction

- Combine all the ingredients.
- Cover and cook over medium-low heat for 30 to 40 minutes or until apples are tender, stirring occasionally.
- Leave chunky (my preference) or mash apples (a potato masher works well) until sauce is desired consistency.
- Serve warm or cold.

249. Copycat Arby's Chicken Salad Recipe

Serving: 0 | Prep: | Cook: 15mins | Ready in:

Ingredients

- 2 C. cubed cooked chicken
- 3/4 C. chopped apple (no need to peel)
- 3/4 C. red seedless grapes, chopped
- 1/2 C. chopped celery
- 1/2 C. chopped pecans
- 3/4 C. mayonnaise
- lettuce leaves
- bread or wraps of choice

Direction

- In a large bowl, combine chicken, apple, grapes, celery, and pecans. Stir in mayonnaise. Place one lettuce leaf on one bread slice. Add chicken salad and top with second bread slice.
- Note: I don't really measure out the ingredient amounts and just eyeball everything. Make as little or as much as desired by reducing or increasing the amounts. The number of servings will also depend on how much you put in each sandwich or wrap. I like to make this early in the day and let it sit in the fridge at least a couple of hours to let the flavors develop.

250. Couscous Salad Recipe

Serving: 8 | Prep: | Cook: 1hours30mins | Ready in:

Ingredients

- 2 cups quick cooking couscous
- 2 1/2 cups water
- 1/4 cup raisins
- 1/4 cup dried apricots, chopped
- 6 tablespoons olive oil
- 4 tablespoons lemon juice
- 2 teaspoons cumin
- 2 teaspoons ground coriander
- 1 teaspoon ground ginger
- 2 teaspoons salt
- 1/4 cup red pepper, diced
- 1/4 cup green onion, sliced
- 2 cups chick peas, rinsed

- 2 tablespoons fresh chopped mint, parsley and cilantro
- 2 tablespoons slivered almonds

Direction

- Soak the raisins and apricots in 1/2 cup boiling water for 1 hour.
- Drain and add to the couscous.
- Pour 2 cups boiling water over the mixture, over and allow water to be absorbed. Cool and fluff with a fork.
- Make a dressing with the oil, lemon juice and spices and mix well.
- In a large bowl combine the couscous with the red pepper, green onions and chickpeas.
- Add the dressing and mix well.
- Toss in the mint, parsley and cilantro.
- Garnish with the almonds.

251.   Crab Apple Salad Recipe

Serving: 4 | Prep: | Cook: | Ready in:

Ingredients

- 1 1/2 cups chopped celery
- 2 cups cooked crab meat (fresh, frozen, or canned) left in good-sized pieces
- 1/2 cup chopped walnuts
- 1 tart apple, cored and cut into slivers (about 1 cup)
- 1/2 cup mayonnaise
- salt, to taste
- lettuce leaves to line bowl or individual dishes (about 4 cups)
- 1 red apple, peel left on, cut into slices
- 1 lemon, cut into 4 wedges

Direction

- Mix together the first six ingredients.
- Cover and chill for several hours.
- When you are ready to eat, place lettuce in serving bowl or 4 individual serving dishes.

- Top with apple slices and lemon slices.
- Serve immediately.
- Squeeze lemon wedges over salad if you wish.

252.   Cran Apple Waldorf Salad

Serving: 8 | Prep: | Cook: | Ready in:

Ingredients

- 1 medium apple, chopped
- 1 celery rib, chopped
- 1/2 cup dried cranberries
- 1/3 cup mayonnaise
- 1 tablespoon sugar
- 2 teaspoons lemon juice

Direction

- In a serving bowl, combine the apple, celery and cranberries. In a small bowl, combine mayonnaise, sugar and lemon juice. Pour over apple mixture and toss gently to coat.
- Nutrition Facts
- 1 cup: 186 calories, 0 fat (0 saturated fat), 0 cholesterol, 295mg sodium, 48g carbohydrate (0 sugars, 5g fiber), 0 protein.

253.   Cranberry Apple Salad Recipe

Serving: 12 | Prep: | Cook: 15mins | Ready in:

Ingredients

- 2 cans whole cranberry sauce
- 2c boiling water
- 2 pkgs(3oz.) strawberry jello
- 2 Tbs lemon juice
- 1/2tsp salt
- 1c light mayonnaise
- 2c diced apples

- 1/2c chopped pecans

Direction

- Melt cranberry sauce over med. heat. Drain, reserving liquid and berries. Mix together cranberry liquid, boiling water and Jell-O. Stir till Jell-O is dissolved. Add lemon juice and salt. Chill until mixture mounds slightly on spoon.
- Add mayonnaise; beat till smooth. Fold in cranberries, apples, and nuts.
- Pour into 2qt. mold. Chill overnight.

---

254.   Cranberry Fruit Salad Recipe

Serving: 0 | Prep: | Cook: 1hours | Ready in:

Ingredients

- CRANBERRY FRUIT SALAD
- Luby's Cafeteria Copycat Recipe
- Serves 8-10
- 1 cup sugar
- 1 cup water
- 1 (12-oz.) package fresh cranberries, washed and picked over
- 1 apple, unpeeled
- 1 orange, peeled and white pith removed
- 1 banana, peeled
- 1 cup broken walnuts or 1 cup pecans

Direction

- In a saucepan, mix sugar and water, stirring to dissolve sugar. Bring to a boil. Add cranberries. Return to a boil, reduce heat and boil gently 4 to 5 minutes or until most cranberries have popped, stirring occasionally. Remove cranberries from heat and cool completely at room temperature. Quarter the apple; core and chop. Add to cool cranberries. Chop the orange and banana and add to cranberries with the nuts. Mix well and

refrigerate until serving time, at least 4 hours or overnight.

---

255.   Cranberry Waldorf Fruit Salad Recipe

Serving: 4 | Prep: | Cook: | Ready in:

Ingredients

- I cup fresh cranberries, chopped
- 1 cup red or green apple, chopped
- 1 cup chopped celery
- 1 cup red or green seedless grapes, halved
- 1/4 cup walnut pieces
- 1/4 tsp cinnamon
- 8 ounces low fat yogurt
- 1/4 to 1/2 tsp vanilla (optional)

Direction

- Add cranberries, apples, celery, grapes and walnuts to medium size serving bowl and toss to mix.
- Add cinnamon and vanilla to yogurt, mix well
- Drizzle over the fruit salad in serving bowl and toss to blend
- Serve immediately

---

256.   Cranberry Waldorf Salad Recipe

Serving: 12 | Prep: | Cook: | Ready in:

Ingredients

- 1 1/2 cups chopped cranberries
- 1 cup chopped unpeeled red apple (can use red and green)
- 1 cup chopped celery
- 1 cup seedless green grapes, halved (can use red and green)

- 1/3 cup raisins
- 1/4 cup chopped walnuts
- 2 tablespoons white sugar
- 1/4 teaspoon ground cinnamon
- 1 (8 ounce) container vanilla low-fat yogurt

Direction

- In a medium bowl, combine cranberries, apple, celery, grapes, raisins, walnuts, sugar, cinnamon, and yogurt.
- Toss to coat. Cover, and chill 2 hours.
- Stir just before serving.

257. Creamy Apple Salad Recipe

Serving: 6 | Prep: | Cook: |Ready in:

Ingredients

- 1-8oz. Cool Whip, fat free
- 1 small box Butterscotch pudding, fat free
- 3 cups apples, bite size pieces
- 1-12oz. can crushed pineapple
- 1 cup miniature marshmallows

Direction

- Mix all ingredients together and refrigerate until ready to serve.

258. Creamy Sugared Grapes Recipe

Serving: 6 | Prep: | Cook: 5mins |Ready in:

Ingredients

- 1 lb. seedless red or green grapes
- 1/2 cup dairy sour cream
- vanilla, optional
- 1/4 cup brown sugar

Direction

- Mix the grapes and sour cream (and small amount of vanilla, optional). Chill for at least one hour.
- Spoon the grape mixture into dessert dishes and sprinkle with the brown sugar.

259. Creamy, Dreamy Grape Salad Recipe

Serving: 10 | Prep: | Cook: 30mins |Ready in:

Ingredients

- 2 lbs. red seedless grapes - remove stems, wash and dry
- 2 lbs. green seedless grapes - remove stems, wash and dry
- 8 oz. cream cheese, softened
- 8 oz. sour cream
- 4 oz. pecans, finely chopped
- 2 Tbsp. light brown sugar
- 1 teas. vanilla

Direction

- The key to this recipe is to make sure the grapes are DRY after washing them or the dressing will be watered down and not stick to the grapes.
- In a large bowl combine softened cream cheese and sour cheese and whip until light and fluffy. Add brown sugar and vanilla and whip a little while until it is incorporated.
- Stir in chopped pecans and grapes. Chill at least 3 hours.
- This is so good you can eat it as a salad or dessert!

260. Crunchy Apple Salad Recipe

Serving: 6 | Prep: | Cook: | Ready in:

Ingredients

- 1 cup diced apples, unpeeled
- 1 cup diced bananas
- 1 Tbsp lemon juice
- 1/2 cup pineapple tidbits, drained
- 1/2 cup raisins (golden raisins are pretty)
- 1/2 cup pecans, coarsely chopped
- 1/3 cup mayonnaise
- lettuce leaves

Direction

- Dice apples first, then bananas.
- Immediately place diced apples and bananas in a bowl and toss with the lemon juice to prevent them from browning.
- Now add pineapple tidbits, raisins and pecans and toss a little, but be gentle so you don't smoosh up the banana pieces.
- Add mayonnaise and mix gently just enough to mix it in.
- Serve over lettuce leaves.

261. Cucumber And Watermelon Salad Recipe

Serving: 6 | Prep: | Cook: 30mins | Ready in:

Ingredients

- 4 C. watermelon, deseeded and either cubed or shaped into balls
- 2 C. english cucumber, sliced
- 3 Tbs. fresh mint, chopped
- 1/4 C. fresh squeezed lime juice
- 1-2 tsp. balsamic vinegar (optional)

Direction

- Take the watermelon, cucumber, mint and lime juice and mix in a bowl.
- Season with salt and pepper to taste.

262. Dot's Waldorf Salad Recipe

Serving: 6 | Prep: | Cook: 10mins | Ready in:

Ingredients

- 4 apples, 2 sweet and 2 tart (I use Granny Smith and Gala) chopped
- juice of 1/2 lemon
- 10 grapes, halved
- 2 stalks celery, chopped
- 1/4-1/3 cup mayonnaise
- 1/4-1/3 cup walnuts
- 1/4 cup raisins (optional)

Direction

- Combine apples and lemon juice
- Add all ingredients and completely combine
- Refrigerate 1 hour before serving

263. Drunken Fruit Salad Recipe

Serving: 6 | Prep: | Cook: 3hours2mins | Ready in:

Ingredients

- 1 medium mango, peeled and cubed
- 1 cup fresh strawberries, hulled and quartered
- 2 kiwis, peeled and cut up
- 1 8 oz can pineapple pieces--only drain about half the juice
- 1 8 oz can mandarin oranges, drained
- rum (amount and flavor up to you--i use coconut rum and put 1/2 a cup in)

Direction

- Mix all together in a large bowl. Chill for a couple of hours before serving.
- Play with the fruit combinations according to your taste! Maybe some blueberries or blackberries yum. I'd avoid using bananas though as they get all squishy and brown.

264. Easy Fruit Salad Recipe

Serving: 6 | Prep: | Cook: 10mins | Ready in:

Ingredients

- 1 large can sliced peaches
- 1 can pineapple chunks
- 1/2 cup blueberries
- 1 1b strawberries, sliced
- 1 cup red seedless grapes
- 2 bananas, sliced
- 1 large pkg vanilla Instant Pudding
- 2 TB sugar

Direction

- In large bowl, add peaches and pineapples, INCLUDING the juices.
- Stir in vanilla pudding mix and sugar until all is dissolved.
- Add remaining fruit and stir to coat well.
- Refrigerate for at least 30 minutes prior to serving.

265. Easy Rose Apple Spicy Salad Recipe

Serving: 2 | Prep: | Cook: 10mins | Ready in:

Ingredients

- INGREDIENTS:
- Mix all the ingredient together

- Place the rose apples and prawn in a bowl
- 5-6 rose apples or any kind of apple sliced
- 100 g. thin slice of steamed prawn meat
- DRESSING INGREDIENTS:
- 1 tbsp. roasted chilli paste
- 2 tbsp. lime juice
- 1 tbsp. ground dried shrimp
- 2 tbsp. water

Direction

- Mixed all the ingredient together
- Place the rose apple and prawn in a bowl
- Pour on the dressing and toss gently.
- Transfer to a plate and enjoy~*

266. Erisian Salad Recipe

Serving: 2 | Prep: | Cook: 15mins | Ready in:

Ingredients

- 4oz orzo
- 2T quality olive oil
- 1 small or 1/2 medium onion, chopped
- 4 cloves garlic, minced
- 1/4 cup banana peppers(hot or mild), sliced*
- 1/4 cup chicken or veggie stock
- 1T fresh lemon juice
- 1/2 cup pitted and chopped kalamata olives
- 1/4 cup chopped peppadews or roasted red peppers
- 6-8 cherry tomatoes, halved or quartered(or, 12-14 grape sized)
- 10-12 green grapes, halved
- 1/4 cup garlic and herb flavored feta cheese, crumbled
- 1/4 cup pine nuts(toasted, preferably)
- 2T capers
- olive oil for frying

Direction

- Cook orzo per package directions.

- Meanwhile, in small pan, sauté onion in 2T olive oil, over medium heat for about 3 minutes
- Add banana peppers (*if using fresh, if jarred, skip this step and add with peppadews/red peppers)
- Continue to cook until onions just begin to caramelize on edges.
- Add stock to hot pan and when sizzling stops, add lemon juice, olives, peppadews/red peppers, tomatoes and banana peppers, if using jarred or canned variety
- Add tomatoes and keep on very low heat
- When pasta is done, rinse with cold water and drain well.
- Immediately add to pan of veggies and stir to combine. Add grapes and stir. At this point, you can either leave it on low to stay warm, remove from heat to serve room temperature, or refrigerate and serve cold.
- When ready to serve, heat 2T olive oil in skillet until water drops "dance" on the oil
- Drain capers well and pat dry on paper towel
- Carefully drop capers in oil (add all at once and stand back! ;) and let them pop and scatter in the pan . They are done when buds are open and capers are lightly crisp
- Remove from oil and drain well.
- To serve salad, top each portion with feta, pine nuts, and fried capers

---

267. Erma's To Die For Fruit & Veggie Salad Recipe

Serving: 6 | Prep: | Cook: 15mins | Ready in:

Ingredients

- a bag of Spring Mix (a bag of specialty greens & baby lettuces)
- a handful of sliced or slivered raw almonds
- a handful of dried cranberries
- 1/4 cup feta or goat cheese
- 1/2 cup chunks of pineapple
- 1/2 cup chunks of melon
- 1/2 cup chunks of ripe mango
- a small sachet of White balsamic vinaigrette
- a handful of steamed shrimp (optional)

Direction

- Toss greens, Almonds, dried Cranberries, & cheese with Vinaigrette until just combined. Set aside.
- Mix fruits together then put on top of the greens. Serve with a big smile. B-)

---

268. Fancy Red Apple Salad Recipe

Serving: 8 | Prep: | Cook: 10mins | Ready in:

Ingredients

- 3 cups red apples, diced
- 2 cups celery, diced
- 1 large can crushed pineapple, drained (reserve juice for dressing)
- 1 cup chopped pecans, medium chop
- 1 cup whipping cream, whipped
- DRESSING:
- juice from pineapple
- 1 egg, beaten
- 3 tablespoons flour
- 3 tablespoons sugar
- 2 tablespoons lemon juice

Direction

- Whisk all dressing ingredients in a pan, stirring constantly, and cook over medium heat until thickened
- Remove from heat and pour into dish to COOL
- When cooled, pour over apples, celery, pineapple, pecans
- Mix well by folding in gently
- Fold in whipped cream
- Refrigerate until time to serve

269. Fantastic Fruit Salad Recipe

Serving: 6 | Prep: | Cook: 30mins | Ready in:

Ingredients

- 1 large can pineapplie chunks (drained)
- 1 container of strawberries (sliced)
- 1 bunch of red grapes (sliced)
- 1 banana (sliced)
- 16 oz sour cream
- milk
- 1 large instant pudding
- 1 can crushed pineapple (drained)

Direction

- Layer chunked pineapple, sliced grapes, sliced strawberries all into bite size pieces (cover and refrigerate).
- Mix together one 16oz sour cream, one large banana cream instant pudding. Then add enough milk until you reach consistency a little thinner then pudding. When you get it how you want it, stir in the crushed pineapple. Cover and refrigerate.
- When ready to serve, slice a banana on top of other fruit, pour in sour cream mixture, stir it up and enjoy.
- Leftovers are only good for about a day as it will get soupy and banana will brown.

270. Fennel And Apple Salad With Blue Cheese Recipe

Serving: 6 | Prep: | Cook: | Ready in:

Ingredients

- 1 ½ tablespoons fresh lemon juice
- 1 ½ teaspoons white wine vinegar
- 1 teaspoon Dijon mustard
- ¼ cup extra-virgin olive oil
- kosher salt and freshly ground black pepper
- 1 large fennel bulb – halved lengthwise, cored and sliced crosswise paper thin
- 1 tablespoon finely chopped fennel fronds
- 1 Granny Smith apple, peeled and cut into matchsticks
- 1 cup crumbled blue cheese (about 4 ounces)
- ¾ cup pecan halves, toasted

Direction

- In a large bowl whisk the lemon juice, vinegar and mustard.
- Gradually whisk in the oil and season with salt and pepper.
- Add the fennel, fennel fronds and apple and season with salt and pepper; toss.
- Garnish with the blue cheese and pecans and serve right away.
- Nice served over arugula if you want some greens. Just dress the greens with some of the dressing.

271. Feta Cheese Apple And Spiced Pecan Salad Recipe

Serving: 8 | Prep: | Cook: 15mins | Ready in:

Ingredients

- 1 head boston lettuce, torn
- 1 head red leaf lettuce, torn
- 1 Red Delicious apple, unpeeled and finely chopped
- 8 ounses feta cheese, crumbled
- spiced pecans
- 1/2 cup oilve oil
- 2 Tbs white wine vinegar
- 1 Tbs plus 1 tsp Dijon mustard
- 1/4 tsp salt
- 1/4 tsp freshly ground pepper

- spiced pecans
- 3 Tbs unsalted butter, melted
- 1 tsp ground cinnamon
- 1/4 tsp ground red pepper
- Dash of hot sauce
- 1 2/3 cups pecan halves

Direction

- Combine lettuce, apple, cheese, and Spiced Pecans in a large bowl
- Toss gently and set aside
- Combine olive oil, vinegar, mustard, salt and pepper in a jar.
- Cover tightly and shake vigorously.
- Pour dressing mixture over lettuce mixture
- Toss gently
- Serve immediately
- Spiced Pecans
- Combine butter, salt, cinnamon, red pepper and hot sauce in a medium bowl
- Add pecans, stirring to coat
- Spread in a single layer on an ungreased baking sheet.
- Bake at 300 degrees for 15 minutes, stirring once
- Cool completely on baking sheet on a wire rack.
- Yield 1 2/3 cups.

272.   Fresh Fruit Salad Recipe

Serving: 6 | Prep: | Cook: 30mins |Ready in:

Ingredients

- 1 fresh pinepapple, peeled cored and cut into chunks
- 3 kiwi fruit peeled and cut into chunks
- 3 oranges peeled and cut into sections and halved
- 3 apples washed and leave skin on, cut into chunks
- 2 bananas, sliced
- 2 c seedless green grapes, halved

- 2 pears, washed and cut into chunks
- 1 c pomegranate seeds (in season)
- 1 c walnuts,optional
- 1 c pear nectar or orange juice

Direction

- Mix all together in a big glass bowl and pour 1 cup of Pear nectar over top coating all fruit.
- Add walnuts just before serving and toss.
- Love this and it can be served alongside pancakes and waffles too with a dollop of whipped cream or Devon cream.

273.   Fresh Peach Salad With Sriracha Vinaigrette Recipe

Serving: 1 | Prep: | Cook: 5mins |Ready in:

Ingredients

- Large fresh peach, pitted and sliced
- 1 green onion sliced on diagonal
- 1/4 cup of crumbled feta
- 6 fresh basil leaves
- Sriracha Vinaigrettte
- 2 tbsp of Sriracha (yes, tablespoons)
- 1 tbsp of honey
- 1 tbsp of red wine vinegar (I added a tiny bit more for extra tang)
- 1/4 tsp of salt
- fresh ground pepper
- 1/4 cup of extra virgin olive oil

Direction

- Whisk dressing ingredients.
- Assemble peach slices, sprinkle with feta, onion and basil.
- Drizzle dressing.
- Enjoy.
- Basil and peach!!! Yummy.

274.   Frozen Apple Salad Recipe

Serving: 9 | Prep: | Cook: 30mins | Ready in:

Ingredients

- Small can crushed pineapple (approx 8 ounces)
- 2 eggs
- 1/2 cup sugar
- 1/8 tsp salt
- 3 Tbsp lemon juice
- 2 cups apples, unpeeled, chopped (2 different colors are pretty)
- 1/2 cup chopped celery
- 1 cup heavy cream
- lettuce leaves

Direction

- Beat eggs.
- Drain pineapple into a measuring cup.
- Add water to the juice to make 1/2 cup liquid.
- Stir liquid into eggs.
- Add sugar, salt and lemon juice.
- On medium burner, cook and stir about 5 minutes, until the mixture thickens.
- Cool.
- When this dressing is cool, whip the heavy cream
- Now fold in the drained pineapple, apple, celery, and whipped cream.
- Spread mixture into a dish or pan that is 8 inches square. Cover and put in freezer until frozen.
- Half an hour before you want to serve, remove from freezer and place in refrigerator for 30 minutes.
- At the end of the 30 minutes, cut in 9 squares and place on lettuce leaves to serve.

275.   Fruit Salad Recipe

Serving: 0 | Prep: | Cook: | Ready in:

Ingredients

- fruit Salad
- 1 (29 ounce) can peach slices
- 1 (20 ounce) can pineapple chunks
- 1 (3 1/8 ounce) box dry vanilla instant pudding mix
- 1 lb of strawberries, (quartered)
- 1 banana, (sliced)
- 1/2 pint blueberries
- 1 bunch grapes (I use the red ones)
- 1 -2 tablespoon sugar (optional)

Direction

- Directions:
- In a large bowl, combine peaches, pineapples, and vanilla pudding mix. This includes the juices from the cans. Mix well until pudding is dissolved. Stir in strawberries, banana, blueberries, grapes, and sugar if desired. Chill.

276.   Fruit Surprise Recipe

Serving: 0 | Prep: | Cook: 5mins | Ready in:

Ingredients

- fruit cocktail with juice
- Box of vanilla pudding
- 1 small Cool Whip

Direction

- Mix the fruit and pudding together
- Fold in the cool whip

277. Fuji Apple Walnut Salad Recipe

Serving: 6 | Prep: | Cook: | Ready in:

Ingredients

- 3 tbsp. packed brown sugar
- 3 tbsp. finely chopped walnuts
- 3 Fuji or any sweet apples, halved and cored
- 1 tbsp. butter, melted
- 1/3 cup canola oil
- 1/4 cup apple cider
- 1/4 cup cider vinegar
- 1 tbsp. honey
- 1/4 tsp. salt
- 1/4 tsp. ground black pepper
- 6 cups spring mixed greens or mesculan
- 1/4 cup coarsely chopped walnuts, toasted

Direction

- Preheat oven to 425F. Line baking sheet with foil; lightly coat with cooking spray.
- In bowl combine brown sugar and finely chopped walnuts.
- Place apple halves, cut sides up, on baking sheet.
- Brush tops of apples with butter; sprinkle with brown sugar nut mixture.
- Bake 15 minutes or until just tender when pierced with a fork.
- Combine oil, cider, vinegar, honey, salt, and pepper. Cover; shake well.
- Arrange greens on serving platter; top with apple halves.
- Spoon melted sugar and walnuts from baking sheet atop salad.
- Pour dressing.
- Sprinkle with coarsely chopped walnut.

278. Gingered Sweet Potato Apple Salad Recipe

Serving: 6 | Prep: | Cook: | Ready in:

Ingredients

- 1 can (15 ounces) sweet potatoes or yams, in light syrup, drained and cubed
- 1 can (8 ounces) pineapple tidbits, in juice, drained
- 1 medium apple, cored and diced
- 1/2 cup diced celery
- 1/2 cup coarsely chopped unsalted cashews
- 1/4 cup honey mustard dressing
- 2 teaspoons freshly grated ginger
- 6 cups mixed salad greens

Direction

- Combine sweet potatoes, pineapple, apple, celery and cashews in a large bowl. In a small bowl, combine honey mustard dressing and ginger; pour over sweet potato mixture; toss lightly. Cover and chill for at least 1 hour. Serve over salad greens.
- Nutritional Information Per Serving: Calories 220; Total fat 7g; Saturated fat 1g; Cholesterol 0mg; Sodium 75mg; Total carbohydrate 37g; Fiber 5g; Protein 4g; Vitamin A 160%DV*; Vitamin C 35%DV; Calcium 6%DV; Iron 15%DV
- * Daily Value
- COURTESY OF MEALTIME.ORG

279. Goat Cheese And Apple Salad Recipe

Serving: 8 | Prep: | Cook: | Ready in:

Ingredients

- 1bag fresh spinach leaves
- 1 granny smith apple (Or your choice of apple)
- 1/2 cup dried cranberries (I use craisins)

- 1/2 - 1 cup glazed pecans
- goat cheese (As much as you want)
- pecan vinaigrette:
- 3 tbl sherry vinegar
- 2 tbl honey
- 1 tbl Dijon mustard
- 2 tbl extravirgin olive oil
- 1/2 tspn salt

Direction

- Make the vinaigrette, set aside.
- In large bowl, toss sliced apple pieces, spinach, cranberries, pecans and goat cheese.
- Pour vinaigrette over salad.

280.   Grandma Bs Apple Salad Recipe

Serving: 8 | Prep: | Cook: 10mins | Ready in:

Ingredients

- 1 Large can crushed pineapple
- 3 Well beaten eggs
- 2 Tablespoons flour
- 1 cup sugar
- 1 Tablespoon butter
- 6 Large crisp red apples
- lemon juice
- 1/2 cups chopped pecans

Direction

- Drain pineapple, reserving juice.
- Dice apples and sprinkle with lemon juice to retain color.
- Bring juice to a boil, carefully add eggs.
- Add flour, sugar, and butter and boil again to thicken.
- Stir well.
- Let cool.
- Add pineapple, diced apples, and pecans.
- Stir well.
- Chill and serve.

281.   Grape Salad Recipe

Serving: 0 | Prep: | Cook: 15mins | Ready in:

Ingredients

- 4 cups seedless red grapes
- 4 cups seedless green grapes
- 8 oz. sour cream
- 8 oz. cream cheese
- 1 tsp. vanilla
- 1/2 cup sugar
- 1/2 cup brown sugar
- 1 cup chopped pecans, optional

Direction

- Mix together sour cream, cream cheese, vanilla, and sugar in a bowl.
- Mix together both types of grapes in a separate bowl.
- Layer grapes in a serving bowl, followed by the sour cream layer. Keep alternating these layers but end with a sour cream layer on top.
- Top the dish with the brown sugar and pecans mixed together.
- Best if chilled overnight

282.   Grape Waldorf Salad Recipe

Serving: 4 | Prep: | Cook: 1mins | Ready in:

Ingredients

- 1/4 Cup sour cream
- 2 Tablespoons brown sugar
- 1 Teaspoon fresh lemon juice
- 1/3 Teaspoon celery seed
- 1/4 Teaspoon salt or to taste
- 1/4 Teaspoon pepper or to taste

- 1/4 Teaspoon cayenne or to taste
- 2 Cups red seedless grapes, halved
- 2 Cups green grapes, halved
- 1/2 Cup celery, diced
- 2 Tablespoons fresh parsley, chopped
- 1/2 Cup pecans, toasted and chopped

Direction

- Whisk together first seven Ingredients to make sauce. Add remaining Ingredients and toss to coat. Let chill one hour, before serving add pecans.

283. Grilled Chicken Waldorf Salad Recipe

Serving: 4 | Prep: | Cook: 10mins | Ready in:

Ingredients

- 2/3 cup sour cream
- 1/4 cup chopped parsley
- 4 teaspoons fresh lime juice
- 2 teaspoons granulated sugar
- 1/4 teaspoon salt
- 4 boneless skinless chicken breast halves
- butter lettuce leaves
- 2 green apples cored and sliced
- 1 cup sliced celery
- 1/2 cup sliced green onions
- 1/4 cup toasted pecans

Direction

- In small bowl mix sour cream, parsley, lime juice, sugar and salt.
- Blend thoroughly then set aside.
- Grill chicken about 8 minutes until juices run clear turning once then keep warm.
- Line 4 dinner plates with lettuce leaves.
- Cut each breast into 1/2-inch slices.
- Arrange chicken, apples and celery on lettuce dividing equally.

- Drizzle with sour cream dressing and sprinkle with onions and pecans.

284. Grilled Fig Salad Recipe

Serving: 4 | Prep: | Cook: 20mins | Ready in:

Ingredients

- 4 large fresh Black Mission or Calimyrna figs
- 2 tablespoons balsamic vinegar
- 2 to 3 teaspoons dark brown sugar
- 1/8 teaspoon ground cinnamon
- 1/4 cup extra virgin olive oil
- 2 to 3 teaspoons freshly squeezed lemon juice
- 1/2 teaspoon Dijon mustard
- sea salt, to taste
- ground pepper, to taste
- 8 cups mixed salad greens

Direction

- Snip the tiny stem end off each fig and cut in half lengthwise. Mix vinegar, brown sugar and cinnamon together in a medium bowl. Add figs and gently toss to coat. Let marinate while you heat a grill (indoor or outdoor).
- If necessary, coat your grill with a little olive oil. When ready, grill the figs, reserving all of the marinade in the bowl, for about 2 to 3 minutes per side or until grill marks appear. Do not overcook as the figs will become too mushy. Remove figs to a plate.
- To the reserved marinade, add olive oil, lemon juice, mustard, salt and pepper, whisking well to completely incorporate.
- Place greens in a large salad bowl. Toss with dressing, then divide among 4 individual serving plates. Place 2 fig halves on each plate of greens and serve.

285. Hazel Briscoe's Cranberry Salad Recipe

Serving: 0 | Prep: | Cook: 15mins | Ready in:

Ingredients

- 2 pkgs any red jello
- 2 cups boiling water
- 1 pkg frozen whole cranberries (about 2 C)
- 1 large orange (seeds removed)
- 2 cups sugar
- 1/2 C pecans (optional) - chopped
- 1/2 C celery - diced

Direction

- Grind cranberries and the orange together, add the sugar, stir and add the add celery and optional pecans. Dissolve jello in boiling water, stir to dissolve completely. Add jello/water mix. Fill a bowl or a mold with the mixture and refrigerate overnight. Can be made 24-48 hours ahead. Place lettuce leaves on a nice plate and then unmold the salad. Serve.

286. Honey Apple Salad Recipe

Serving: 6 | Prep: | Cook: | Ready in:

Ingredients

- 3 1/2 cups diced red apples
- 2 tbs lemon juice
- 2 cups green seedles grapes
- 1 cup thin sliced celery
- 1/2 cup chopped dates
- 1/2 cup mayo
- 1/4 cup honey
- 2 tbs sour cream
- dash salt
- 1/2 cup chopped walnuts

Direction

- Toss apple with lemon juice
- Add grapes, celery and dates
- Combine mayo, honey, sour cream and salt and mix well
- Pour over apples and mix gently
- Stir in the nuts
- Serve immediately

287. Hot Apple Salad On Grilled Halloumi Recipe

Serving: 8 | Prep: | Cook: 10mins | Ready in:

Ingredients

- Salad
- 8 oz halloumi, sliced about 1/4" thick**
- 1 med granny smith apple, peeled and cored
- 1 med fuji apple, peeled and cored
- 1/2 cup golden raisins
- 1/2 habanero, finely diced
- 2 tbsp lemon juice
- 1 tbsp butter
- Pinch ground cloves
- Microgreens
- olive oil
- Fresh mint sprigs for garnish
- Dressing:
- 1/2 c plain yogurt
- 1-2 tbsp lemon juice
- 1/3 cup finely slivered mint leaves
- 2 tsp honey
- salt and white pepper to taste
- **Halloumi typically comes shaped like a block of tofu. You can slice from the end if you like for long, thin strips. I prefer to slice from the "top" for larger squares.

Direction

- Matchstick peeled and cored apples. Place in a bowl of cold water with 2 tbsp. lemon juice and set aside.

116

- Meanwhile bring a small pot of water to a low boil. Add raisins and remove from heat. Allow raisins to steep and plump for at least 10 minutes.
- While raisins are steeping, combine all dressing ingredients and season to taste. Adjust consistency to preference with lemon juice and allow to chill until serving.
- Heat 1 tbsp. butter in a heavy skillet over medium-high heat. Strain apples and add to melted butter, tossing well to coat. Add raisins, diced habanero, and a teeny pinch of ground cloves and cook 7-9 minutes or until apples are tender crisp and lightly golden. Remove from heat and keep warm.
- Preheat grill or indoor grill pan and arrange micro greens on 8 beautiful salad plates.
- Lightly brush sliced halloumi with olive oil on each side and place on hot grill, cooking for 1-2 minutes or until just marked and warm. Flip and repeat.
- Evenly divide halloumi among salad plates beside and on top of micro greens. Divide apple salad into even portions and spoon over each plate.
- Drizzle with yogurt mint dressing. Garnish with fresh mint and serve immediately.

288.   Hot Fruit Salad Recipe

Serving: 8 | Prep: | Cook: 1hours | Ready in:

Ingredients

- 16 oz can sliced peaches, drained
- 16 oz can pear halves, drained and chopped
- 16 oz can plums, drained and pitted
- 16 oz can apricot halves, drained
- 16 oz jar spiced apple rings, drained
- 20 oz can pineapple chunks, drained
- 6 oz jar cherries, drained
- 16 oz applesauce
- 6 T margarine
- 3/4 c firmly packed brown sugar

- 1/2 tsp cinnamon
- 1/2 tsp allspice
- 1/2 c chopped walnuts or pecans

Direction

- Combine first 7 ingredients; spread in 13x9 dish.
- Combine applesauce, margarine, brown sugar and spices in saucepan; heat thoroughly. Spoon over fruit; sprinkle with nuts. Bake at 300 for 45 minutes.

289.   Jello Waldorf Salad Recipe

Serving: 8 | Prep: | Cook: | Ready in:

Ingredients

- 6 ounces raspberry gelatin powder
- 2 cups boiling water
- 1 cup cold water
- 1 cup lemon-lime soda
- 4 cups apples; peeled and grated
- 1/2 cup celery; diced fine
- 1/2 cup walnuts; chopped

Direction

- In a large bowl, dissolve gelatin in boiling water, then add cold water and soda.
- Refrigerate until syrupy and partially set.
- Fold in remaining ingredients until well mixed.
- Chill until set.

290.   Jeweled Kale And Cabbage Salad Recipe

Serving: 6 | Prep: | Cook: 15mins | Ready in:

Ingredients

- [Section] Salad [/section]
- 1/4 cup dried cranberries (or cherries)
- orange juice or lemonade – enough to cover dried fruit
- 3 cups shredded kale
- 3 cups shredded cabbage
- 1/4 cup toasted pine nuts
- 1/4 cup shaved Parmesan Reggiano asiago cheeses
- [Section] Dressing [/section]
- 1 tbsp Creole or other grainy mustard
- 3 tbsp lemon juice
- 1 tbsp + 1 tsp maple syrup
- 2 tbsp olive oil
- sea salt and black pepper, freshly grated – to taste

Direction

- [Section] Salad [/section]
- The day before you plan to make this salad, combine dried cranberries and juice in a small container. Seal and let sit overnight to reconstitute the fruit.
- Preheat oven to 425F. Spread shredded kale and cabbage out on lined baking sheets giving room so as not to crowd.
- Bake kale and cabbage for 6 minutes. Transfer from baking sheets to a large mixing bowl.
- Add reconstituted cranberries, pine nuts, and cheese. Toss with dressing and serve.
- [Section] Dressing [/section]
- Combine mustard, lemon juice, maple syrup in a small non-reactive bowl. Whisk to incorporate. Add olive oil and whisk to emulsify. Season to taste with salt and pepper.

---

291. Joan's Berry Yummy Salad Recipe

Serving: 1 | Prep: | Cook: 10mins |Ready in:

Ingredients

- arugula
- romaine lettuce
- boston lettuce
- sliced fresh strawberries
- fresh raspberries
- seedless orange chunks
- walnut or pecan pieces
- crumbled feta

Direction

- Clean and pat dry enough arugula, romaine, and Boston lettuce to make the number of salads you are wanting. Rip all three greens into nice small pieces and place in bowls. Add the sliced strawberries, raspberries and orange chunks and then sprinkle the nut pieces and the crumbled feta over the top. Serve with a fruity dressing. Enjoy! :)

---

292. Kaleslaw Salad Recipe

Serving: 8 | Prep: | Cook: 20mins |Ready in:

Ingredients

- apple cider vinaigrette
- 1/3 cup olive oil
- 3 T. apple cider vinegar
- 2 T. lemon juice
- 2 T. orange juice
- 2 T. Dijon mustard
- 2 T. maple syrup
- The Salad
- 4 cups kale (I have found baby kale in the stores lately)
- 2 cups red cabbage, chopped
- 2 cups carrots, grated
- 1 cup dried cranberries
- 3/4 cup pumpkin seeds (pepitas)
- 1/2 cup scallions, sliced
- (1/3 cup chopped fresh parsley)

Direction

- Combine all the dressing ingredients and set aside. (Make a day before serving)
- Toss all the salad ingredients together. Pour on dressing to taste.
- Enjoy!

---

293. Kicked Up Ambrosia Salad Recipe

Serving: 12 | Prep: | Cook: 10mins | Ready in:

Ingredients

- 1 pint fresh blackberries, rinsed and hulled
- 1 pint fresh raspberries, rinsed and hulled
- 1/2 pint fresh strawberries, rinsed and quartered(I used the whole pint)
- 2 large bananas, peeled and cut into 1/4-inch slices
- 2 medium oranges, peeled and cut into segments
- 2 cups medium diced fresh pineapple
- 1 lemon, juiced
- 2 tablespoons chiffonade fresh mint leaves
- 1/2 cup granulated sugar
- 2 cups heavy cream
- 1/2 cup sifted confectioners' sugar
- 1 teaspoon pure vanilla extract
- 1 cup coconut flakes, toasted

Direction

- In a large bowl, combine all the fruit.
- Add the lemon juice, mint and sugar.
- Mix well and set aside.
- In a cold bowl of an electric mixer, combine the cream, sugar and vanilla. Using an electric mixer fitted with a whip attachment or hand-held mixer, whip the cream until soft peaks form.
- To assemble, spoon some of the fruit mixture in the bottom of each parfait or martini glass.
- Sprinkle some of the coconut over the fruit.

- Spoon some of the whipped cream over the coconut.
- Continue layering until all of the ingredients are used.
- Serve immediately or chill until ready to serve.
- Note: I layered fruit, cream and coconut in a glass bowl and garnished with mint and strawberries

---

294. Lemony Light Waldorf Salad Recipe

Serving: 2 | Prep: | Cook: 15mins | Ready in:

Ingredients

- 1/2 cup raw honey or agave
- juice of one small lemon
- 4 cups of mixed red and romaine lettuce, chopped
- 2 ripe red apples, any variety, chopped
- 3 wands of celery, diced
- 2 cups of red or green grapes
- 1 cup of raw walnuts, soaked and drained

Direction

- Combine honey and lemon in large mixing bowl and whisk together until well incorporated. Place remaining ingredients in bowl and mix gently until everything is coated with dressing. Transfer to salad plates and dust with cinnamon.

---

295. Light Waldorf Salad Recipe

Serving: 8 | Prep: | Cook: | Ready in:

Ingredients

- 2 lbs apples peeled and sliced

- 4 Tbs honey
- 4 Cups chopped celery
- 3/4 Cup walnuts chopped
- 4 cups grapes (optional
- 1/2 Cup Low cal Mayonaise
- 3 1/2 Cups lemon or vanilla yogurt

Direction

- Chop up apples, celery and walnuts.
- Combine Honey, Mayo and Yogurt.
- Add this dressing to fruit, celery and walnuts.
- Chill for an hour to allow flavors to blend.
- Serve.

296. Lucie's Ruby Red And Caraway Salad Recipe

Serving: 4 | Prep: | Cook: 10mins | Ready in:

Ingredients

- 8 oz Ruby red grapefruit sections , peeled. If you are a Costco member they have cups of these ready to use - so handy and great
- 1 whole avocado, divided into chunks or slices (optional)
- 4 cups Romaine or bibb lettuce
- Poppy seed or oil and vinegar dressing
- 1/4 tsp caraway seed - or to taste

Direction

- You can either:
- A) Arrange lettuce and the fruit on individual plates and then garnish with caraway seeds and drizzle over the dressing
- - or-
- B) Put all ingredients into a big salad bowl and enough dressing to coat it and toss
- Chill for 30 minutes and serve - chilling is nice, this salad is best chilled.
- It's better than you can imagine, the caraway really is wonderful and it's never failed to be perfect with almost any meal.

297. Mango Chicken Salad Recipe

Serving: 1 | Prep: | Cook: 10mins | Ready in:

Ingredients

- 1 small or 1/2 large chicken breast, grilled
- 2 cups chopped romaine
- 1/3 small can, mandarin oranges
- 1/4 mango, sliced into pieces about 1/4 inch thick
- 1 1/2 tablespoons craisins
- 1/4 cup pecans, coarsely chopped or broken into pieces
- 2 teaspoons crystallized ginger
- honey mustard salad dressing

Direction

- 1. Top romaine with orange slices, mango, Craisins, pecans and crystallized ginger (don't leave this out; it seems to disappear but the taste is noticeable.
- 2. Cut the chicken breast into slices about 1/4 inch thick and put it on top.
- 3. Serve the salad dressing on the side and add it to taste (I used Johnny Fleeman's Gourmet dressing from Walmart and though it was excellent).

298. Mango Cocktail Salad Recipe

Serving: 6 | Prep: | Cook: 20mins | Ready in:

Ingredients

- 2 mangoes, peeled and cubed
- 2 avocados, peeled and cubed
- 1/2 cup walnut pieces

- 1/2 head iceberg lettuce, shredded
- 1/2 medium red onion, very thinly sliced
- for the creamy parsley dressing:
- 1 clove garlic, crushed
- 1 teaspoon Italian parsley, finely chopped
- 1 teaspoon Dijon mustard
- 2 tablespoons lemon juice
- 1/4 cup olive oil

Direction

- To make the dressing: put all ingredients in a small food processor and process until thick. Or you can put mustard and garlic in a mixing bowl and gradually whisk in the olive oi to form a dressing. Mix in parsley and lemon juice and season to taste with salt and pepper.
- Gently combine the mango and avocado cubes and the red onion with the dressing. Serve over the shredded lettuce and sprinkle with walnut pieces right before you serve. (Or you can put the lettuce on a platter and spoon the mixture over the lettuce - it makes a pretty presentation for a group.)

299.   Mango Slaw With Cashews And Mint Recipe

Serving: 0 | Prep: | Cook: 45mins | Ready in:

Ingredients

- 2 mangoes, peeled, pitted and julienned
- 1 to 1 1/4 pounds napa cabbage, halved and sliced very thinly
- 1 red pepper, julienned
- 1/2 red onion, thinly sliced
- 6 T of fresh lime juice, from about two limes
- 1/4 c rice vinegar
- 2 t oil of your choice
- 1/2 t salt
- 1/4 t red pepper flakes, or to taste (or omit this and whisk in a chile paste to taste)
- 1/4 c thinly sliced fresh mint leaves
- 1/4 c toasted cashews, coarsely chopped

Direction

- Toss mangoes, cabbage, pepper and onion in a large bowl.
- Whisk lime juice, vinegar, oil, salt and red pepper in a smaller bowl and pour over slaw.
- You can either serve this immediately or leave the flavors to muddle for an hour in the fridge. Before serving, toss with mint leaves and sprinkle with cashews.

300.   Massaged Kale Salad Recipe

Serving: 4 | Prep: | Cook: 20mins | Ready in:

Ingredients

- 1 bunch kale, stalks removed and discarded, leaves thinly sliced
- 1 lemon juiced
- 1/4 cup extra-virgin olive oil, plus extra for drizzling
- salt
- 2 tsp honey
- Freshly ground black pepper
- 1 mango, diced small (about 1 cup)
- Small handful toasted pepitas (pumpkin seeds)

Direction

- In large serving bowl, add the kale, half of lemon juice, a drizzle of oil and a little salt. Massage until the kale starts to soften & wilt, 2-3 minutes. Set aside while making the dressing.
- In a small bowl, whisk remaining lemon juice with the honey and lots of freshly ground pepper. Stream in the 1/4 cup oil while whisking until a dressing forms, and you like how it tastes.
- Pour the dressing over the kale, add the mango & pepitas. Toss & Serve.

301. Mint And Apple Lamb With Crunchy Salad Recipe

Serving: 4 | Prep: | Cook: 10mins | Ready in:

Ingredients

- 8 lamb cutlets
- olive oil
- 1 cup of apple juice
- 1/4 cup of fresh finely chopped mint leaves
- sea salt and cracked pepper
- 150g snow peas- trimmed
- 1 bunch radishes, finely sliced
- 2 stalks celery, trimmed and finely sliced

Direction

- Heat a large non-stick frying pan over high heat.
- Brush the lamb chops with olive oil and cook for 2 - 3 minutes on each side.
- Set aside and keep warm.
- Reduce the heat to medium.
- Place the apple juice, mint, salt and pepper in a bowl and stir to combine.
- Slowly add the apple mixture to the pan and cook for 3 - 4 minutes or until slightly reduced.
- Thinly slice the snow peas and place in a bowl with the radish and celery and toss to combine.
- Spoon over the apple and mint sauce and serve the crunchy salad with the lamb cutlets.

302. Minted Melon Salad Recipe

Serving: 8 | Prep: | Cook: 15mins | Ready in:

Ingredients

- about 6 cups fresh melon pieces(probably about 1 cantaloupe and 1 honey dew, or half a watermelon and 1 other melon or 1 personal watermelon and another honeydew or cantaloupe...:)
- 2 cups grapes(I used the large red grapes...not seedless. We just eat 'em whole, seeds and all, anyway ;)
- For Dressing
- juice from 3 fresh limes(about 2 1/2-3T)
- 1/4 cup honey
- 1t vanilla
- 1t kosher or sea salt
- about 5 medium/large fresh mint leaves, chopped

Direction

- Place fruit in large bowl and sprinkle with salt. Toss and let rest while preparing dressing.
- For Dressing
- Whisk together lime juice, honey and vanilla until well combined.
- Add about 1 1/2T fresh mint leaves to dressing
- Pour over fruit and toss, again, to coat.
- Refrigerate at least 1 hour, if possible to chill and let flavors meld.
- Add additional fresh mint just before serving, if desired.
- Can also be served in the halves of the melons, used! :)

303. Mixed Green Salad With Diced Avocado, Peaches, Crispy Bacon, Feta Cheese And Champagne Vinaigrette Recipe

Serving: 4 | Prep: | Cook: 15mins | Ready in:

Ingredients

- 1/4 cup champagne vinegar
- 1 tablespoon honey
- 2 teaspoons minced shallots
- 1/2 teaspoon Dijon mustard

- 1/4 teaspoon minced garlic
- 1/2 cup extra-virgin olive oil
- salt and fresh ground black pepper
- 1/2 pound mixed greens
- 1 cup diced ripe peaches
- 1/2 avocado, diced
- 4 strips bacon, cooked until crispy and crumbled
- 1/3 cup feta cheese

Direction

- In a blender, combine the champagne vinegar, honey, shallots, mustard and garlic. Puree until smooth, 10 to 15 seconds. While continuing to blend, slowly drizzle the olive oil into the blender through the opening in the lid until the dressing is smooth and emulsified. Season with salt and pepper to taste and transfer to a clean, non-reactive container with a lid. Set aside until ready to use, or store in the refrigerator for up to 1 week.
- To make the salad, in a large stainless steel bowl, combine the mixed greens, peaches, avocado, bacon and feta cheese. Drizzle about 1/2 cup of the vinaigrette into the bowl and season with salt and pepper. Toss the salad gently but thoroughly to combine, then serve immediately on chilled salad plates.

---

304. Orange Jicama Kale Salad Recipe

Serving: 8 | Prep: | Cook: 20mins | Ready in:

Ingredients

- Dressing ingredients:
- 1 teaspoon extra virgin olive oil
- 1 teaspoon toasted sesame oil
- Zest of 1 lime
- Juice of 1 lime
- ½ tablespoon brown sugar

- 1 teaspoon fish sauce (sold in the Asian section of your grocery store)
- 1 whole jalapeno pepper, seeds and veins removed, and diced
- Salad ingredients:
- 2 large navel oranges, peeled and diced
- 1 small jicama, peeled and diced
- ½ cup or more (depending on your likes) chopped kale (leaves only - discard the stems)
- ¼ cup chopped cilantro

Direction

- Whisk all dressing ingredients together in a small bowl; set aside.
- Combine all salad ingredients in a large bowl, mix to combine.
- Drizzle dressing over all; toss to coat.
- Keep chilled until ready to serve.

---

305. Pale Peach Perfection Salad Recipe

Serving: 3 | Prep: | Cook: 15mins | Ready in:

Ingredients

- 1 bag of pre-washed baby spinach leaves
- 1 large white flesh peach
- 1/3 cup of crumbled fresh feta cheese
- 1/4 cup of slivered almonds, toasted
- 1/2 teaspoon of cajun seasoning blend
- 1 1/2 tbsp white balsamic vinegar
- 1 tbsp Dijon mustard
- 1 tbsp honey
- 1/3 to 1/2 cup of extra virgin olive oil

Direction

- Whisk vinegar, mustard and honey together.
- Add Cajun seasoning.
- Whisk in olive oil until dressing emulsifies.
- Slice peach into thin slivers.
- Top baby spinach with peach, feta and almonds.

- Toss and EAT!

---

306. Papaya Salad Recipe

Serving: 0 | Prep: | Cook: 20mins | Ready in:

Ingredients

- 1 green pawpaw/papaya
- 1 onion
- coconut oil
- salt
- pepper
- Peri-peri Chilli or any sort you prefer
- juice of 1 lemon

Direction

- Peel the pawpaw/papaya. Cut in lengthwise and remove the seeds. Wash the pawpaw/papaya well in water. Grate the pawpaw/papaya. Slice the onions and crush the chili. Heat oil in a pan and fry the onions, next add the grated pawpaw/papaya and stir well now. Add chili and continue stirring for another 5 mins. Squeeze in the lemon juice and season with salt and pepper. Remove from heat.

---

307. Party Apple Salad Recipe

Serving: 6 | Prep: | Cook: 10mins | Ready in:

Ingredients

- 3 apples, cored and diced
- 2 cups of diced celery
- 1 med. can of crushed pineapple, drained (reserve juice)
- 1 cup chopped nuts (I like pecans for this dish)
- 1 cup whipping cream, whipped
- Dressing:
- juice from pineapple

- 1 egg
- 3 tablespoons flour
- 3 tablespoons sugar
- 2 tablespoons lemon juice

Direction

- Boil dressing ingredients just until thickened. Pour over apples, celery, pineapple, and nuts; mix well and let cool. Fold in whipped cream. Chill before serving.

---

308. Pat Nixon's California Fruit Salad Recipe

Serving: 2 | Prep: | Cook: 15mins | Ready in:

Ingredients

- 8 oz nonfat plain yogurt
- 2 tbsp thawed orange juice concentrate
- 2 tbsp mint leaves
- 1 tbsp honey
- 1 small head of iceberg lettuce cut into 8 wedges
- 1 small can mandarin oranges, drained
- 6 fresh peaches, halved and pits removed
- 1 pint fresh strawberries, sliced in half
- 1 cantaloupe (seeded, sliced, and rind removed)
- 1/2 cup shelled and chopped pistachios
- Combine yogurt, orange juice, honey, and mint for dressing.

Direction

- To assemble salad, on individual serving plates place a wedge of lettuce on each plate. Place remaining fruit over lettuce wedges on each plate. Drizzle dressing on top or serve to the side.

309. Peach And Walnut Summer Salad Recipe

Serving: 8 | Prep: | Cook: 10mins |Ready in:

Ingredients

- Dressing
- 1/3 cup walnuts, toasted
- 1/2 cup chopped peaches
- 1/4 cup orange juice
- 1 tablespoon lemon or lime juice
- Salad
- 1 head green leaf lettuce, leaves washed and torn into bite-size pieces
- 1 head red leaf lettuce, leaves washed and torn into bite-size pieces
- 2 peaches, halved, pitted and thinly sliced
- 8 radishes, thinly sliced
- 1 cucumber, halved lengthwise and thinly sliced
- 1/2 cup walnuts, toasted

Direction

- Put all dressing ingredients in a food processor or high-powered blender and puree until smooth. Add a little water if needed to thin to a pourable consistency.
- Toss salad ingredients in a large bowl. Drizzle with dressing, toss to coat well and serve immediately.

310. Pina Colada Salad Recipe

Serving: 0 | Prep: | Cook: 1hours |Ready in:

Ingredients

- 2 cups of cold milk
- 1 can frozen pina colada mix
- 1/2 c. pineapple juice
- 1 small pkg. instant vanilla pudding
- 1 small pkg. instant coconut cream pudding
- 1) 20 oz. can crushed pineapple; drained
- 2 cups shredded coconut
- 8 oz. whipped topping

Direction

- Combine milk, Pina colada mix, and pineapple juice. Add puddings
- - beat 5 minutes. Fold in all other ingredients. Chill several hours.
- Can garnish each serving with pineapple chunks ñ maraschino cherries.

311. Pineapple Basil Salad Recipe

Serving: 6 | Prep: | Cook: 1hours |Ready in:

Ingredients

- 1/2 cup stevia granular sweetener
- 1/2 cup water
- 1/2 cup packed basil leaves
- 1 tablespoon lime peel, grated
- 4 cups fresh pineapple, cubed
- 3 cups fresh strawberries, quartered
- 1/2 cup fresh blueberries

Direction

- Combine sweetener with ½ cup water in a saucepan; bring to a boil.
- Cook 1 minute or until sweetener dissolves.
- Remove from heat and stir in basil and lime peel.
- Cool to room temperature then strain through a fine strainer into a bowl; discard solids.
- Combine pineapple, strawberries and blueberries in a large bowl.
- Drizzle with Splenda mixture and toss to coat.
- Chill until ready to serve.

312.   Pineapple Macaroni Salad Recipe

Serving: 12 | Prep: | Cook: 10mins |Ready in:

Ingredients

- 1/2 pkg raw macaroni cooked and drained
- 1/2 pkg wacky mac (vegetable pasta)cooked and drained
- 1/2 carton cherry tomatoes chopped coarsely
- 1 small carrot finely chopped
- 1 stalk celery finely chopped
- 2 Tbs fine chopped red onion
- 2 Tbs fresh chopped parsley
- 1 Tbs fresh chopped cilantro
- 1/2 cup fresh pineapple chopped into bite size pieces
- mayonnaise to bind
- salt and pepper to taste

Direction

- Drain, rinse and cool pasta
- Place in a large bowl with prepared chopped vegetables and pineapple
- Blend in enough Mayonnaise to bind
- Season to taste with salt and pepper
- Decorate with additional fresh pineapple if desired
- Chill if desired and serve

313.   Pomelo Spicy Salad Recipe

Serving: 0 | Prep: | Cook: 30mins |Ready in:

Ingredients

- 2 cups pomelo fresh peeled
- ½ cup thin slices of shelled steamed prawn
- ¼ cup pan-roasted shredded coconut meat
- ¼ cup coarsely ground pan-roasted peanut
- 1 tbsp. sauted shallot slices
- 1 thinly sliced red spur chilli
- 1 tsp. thinly sliced kaffir lime leaves
- 1 tbsp. coriander leaves
- DRESSING INGREDIENTS
- 1 dried large chilli, roasted until fragrant
- 1 tbsp. well-pounded dried knife fish
- 2 roasted shallots, 1 roasted garlic bulb
- 3 tbsp. palm sugar, 3 tbsp. fish sauce
- 3 tbsp. tamarind juice

Direction

- DRESSING COOKING:
- Pound the chili, fish, shallots and garlic until well ground. Transfer to a pot, add the fish sauce, sugar and tamarind juice and simmer until thickened.
- PREPARATION:
- Place the pomelo in a bowl, add the prawn and then pour on the dressing. Add the coconut, the peanuts, and half a tablespoonful of the sautéed shallot and toss gently until thoroughly mixed.
- Transfer the salad onto a plate, sprinkle with the remaining sautéed shallot, spur chili, kaffir lime leaves and the coriander leaves and then serve.

314.   Porcupine Fruit Salad Recipe

Serving: 30 | Prep: | Cook: 1hours |Ready in:

Ingredients

- 1 large watermelon
- 1 green apple
- 1 red apple
- 1 cantalope
- 2 pints blueberries
- 1 pint strawberries
- 1 nectarine
- 1 plum
- 1 peach
- 15 cherries, pitted

- bunch of greenor purple grapes
- 30-40 toothpicks

Direction

- Carve out the watermelon
- Cut up fruit
- Put fruit inside shell of watermelon
- Add toothpicks :)
- Add cherries for eyes and nose

315.   Pretty In Pink Shredded Beet And Apple Salad Recipe

Serving: 0 | Prep: | Cook: 12mins | Ready in:

Ingredients

- 1/2 green apple, shredded w. a mandolin
- 3/4 cup shredded pickled beets from a jar - i used Pulaski
- chopped toasted walnuts- about 1/4 cup- to taste
- crumbled blue cheese, i used stilton- about 1/4 cup- to taste
- 1/3 cup cooked barley
- raisins- a small handful- to taste
- kosher salt and freshly cracked blk pepper to taste

Direction

- Shred apple over a medium sized bowl.
- Add the rest of the ingredients, stirring after each to incorporate.
- Adjust quantities to taste.
- Enjoy!

316.   Radicchiolously Delizioso Asparagus Salad With Cherry Dijon Dressing Recipe

Serving: 2 | Prep: | Cook: 20mins | Ready in:

Ingredients

- For Salad
- 10oz mixed Italian greens like Romaine, arugula, radicchio, etc
- 8-10 fresh asparagus spears, tops only(about 2 inches down)
- 1T olive oil
- sea salt
- 4oz gourmet roll(not sliced) salami(look in your grocer's specialty case)
- 4oz Fontina cheese, shredded(this should yield about 1/2 cup)
- 12-16 fresh sweet cherries
- 2 green onions sliced
- For Croutons
- 4 thick(1/2") cut pieces from Italian bread loaf(garlic and herb, if possible) cut into thirds
- 1/2 stick butter
- --if using plain Italian bread, add the following:
- 2 cloves garlic
- 1t fresh Italian herbs, chopped(basil +/- oregano)
- For Dressing
- 1 rounded T cherry all fruit preserves/spread
- 1T Dijon
- 3-4T balsamic vinegar
- 1/4 cup dressing quality olive oil
- 1t fresh Italian herbs, chopped fine
- season salt blend
- extra fresh ground black pepper

Direction

- For Salad
- Toss asparagus tops in 1T olive oil and place in broiler safe pan (I use cast iron)
- Sprinkle with sea salt
- Broil about 5 minutes until al dente and still bright green color, and set aside

- Cut cherries in half by placing knife in stem end, and rotating cherry without picking up the knife, until you are all around the cherry(similarly to how it is recommended to cut open avocados)
- Gently "twist" cherry and it will open, again, like an avocado, with the pit staying in one side
- Carefully pop pit out with end of dull knife or baby spoon
- Slice salami into 8 slices, then cut those slices into quarters
- For Croutons
- Melt butter in medium glass bowl in microwave
- Carefully toss bread pieces in butter (and herbs, if using) until all pieces are coated and butter is gone
- Place on baking tray or oven safe pan (I used the SAME cast iron as I did for the asparagus, and the salt at the bottom lent a great flavor :) and bake for about 15 minutes at 350.
- Croutons should be crunchy and golden brown all around with a slight give in the middles
- Set aside
- For Dressing
- In small glass bowl, combine preserves, Dijon, vinegar, herbs, salt and pepper and whisk well
- Slowly add oil, whisking constantly, to emulsify and combine well.
- Taste and adjust as needed
- To Plate Salad
- Lay down a bed of greens
- Top with asparagus, salami, cherries and green onion
- Add cheese and croutons and drizzle with dressing

Serving: 4 | Prep: | Cook: 15mins | Ready in:

Ingredients

- For Salad:
- 3 cups romaine lettuce, torn
- 1 cup English cucumber, chopped
- 2 scallions, chopped
- 1/2 cup yellow bell pepper, chopped
- 1/2 cup red bell pepper, chopped
- 1 large carrot, peeled and sliced thin diagonally
- 1 Granny Smith apple, cored and sliced thin
- 1 cup fresh blueberries
- 1/2 cup walnuts
- 2/3 cup feta cheese (I use a Mediteranean Herb flavord feta)
- For Dressing:
- 3 tbsp. apple cider vinegar
- 2 tbsp fresh lemon juice
- 2 tsp. dijon mustard
- 2 tsp. honey
- 1/2 tsp onion powder
- 1/4 tsp kosher salt
- 1/2 cup grapeseed oil
- 2 tbsp poppy seeds

Direction

- Toss lettuce, cucumber, scallions, bell pepper and carrot together. Arrange apple slices on top and sprinkle with blueberries, walnuts and feta cheese.
- To prepare dressing, whisk together vinegar, lemon juice, mustard, honey, onion powder and salt. Slowly drizzle in oil, whisking constantly, until combined. Stir in poppy seeds.
- Pour over salad and serve.

318. Red Cabbage And Apple Salad Recipe

Serving: 8 | Prep: | Cook: 5mins | Ready in:

Ingredients

- 1 qt shredded red cabbage
- 1 cup apples, quartered & sliced thin
- 1 tsp salt
- 2 Tbsp brown sugar
- 2 Tbsp vinegar
- 3 Tbsp butter
- 1/2 tsp mustard
- 1/2 cup sour cream
- pepper to taste

Direction

- Melt the butter in a saucepan, add the cabbage and apple and stir until the butter coats the mixture and there are signs of softening, but the mixture is not really cooked.
- Add the vinegar, sugar, seasonings and mustard; simmer another 2 minutes the stir in the sour cream. Serve hot.

319. Red, White And Greens With Spicy Lime Dressing Recipe

Serving: 6 | Prep: | Cook: 10mins | Ready in:

Ingredients

- 1 bag mixed baby greens
- 6oz goat cheese(Chevre), crumbled
- 1pt fresh strawberries, hulled and sliced
- 2 green onions, sliced
- 1/2 cup flavored almonds(I used chili lime made by Planters, but you could also use a sweet variety, if you'd rather)
- Spicy Lime Dressing
- 1/2 cup dressing quality olive oil
- 2 limes(juice and zest)

- 2T honey
- 1tsp chili powder
- 1tsp cumin
- 1/2-1tsp cayenne(to taste)
- 2 cloves garlic, minced
- salt and pepper

Direction

- Combine all dressing ingredients other than oil in medium glass bowl.
- Whisk to combine.
- Slowly add olive oil, whisking constantly, to incorporate.
- Arrange greens on individual plates or large serving dish. Top with sliced strawberries and green onions.
- Add crumbled goat cheese and top with almonds
- Dress just before serving
- This dressing is the same as one I created for a friend, only doubled and cayenne added. That recipe can be seen, here. Kenis Spicy Lime Salad Dressing

320. Roasted Apple And Cheddar Salad Recipe

Serving: 6 | Prep: | Cook: 40mins | Ready in:

Ingredients

- Dressing:
- 3 tablespoons red-wine vinegar
- 2 tablespoons apple juice
- 1 tablespoon extra-virgin olive oil
- 1 tablespoon honey
- 2 teaspoons Dijon mustard
- 1/8 teaspoon salt
- Freshly ground pepper to taste
- Salad:
- 2 apples, peeled and cut into wedges
- 2 teaspoons plus 1 tablespoon extra-virgin olive oil

- 4 sprigs fresh thyme or 1/4 teaspoon dried
- 1/4 cup chopped walnuts
- 3 cups baby spinach or torn spinach leaves
- 3 cups torn boston lettuce
- 3 cups torn curly endive
- 2/3 cup grated sharp cheddar cheese

Direction

- Preheat oven to 400°F.
- Prepare dressing: Whisk vinegar, apple juice, 1 tablespoon oil, honey, mustard, salt and pepper in a small bowl.
- Roast apples & prepare salad: Toss apples with 2 teaspoons oil and thyme in a medium bowl; spread evenly on a baking sheet. Roast, turning once or twice, until the apples are soft and golden, 25 to 30 minutes. Discard fresh thyme, if using. Let cool.
- While the apples are roasting, toast walnuts in a small baking pan until fragrant, about 5 minutes. Let cool.
- Before serving, combine spinach, lettuce and endive in a large bowl; toss gently to mix. Divide the greens among 6 plates, drizzle with dressing and top with cheese, roasted apples and walnuts. Serve immediately.

---

321.   Roasted Butternut Squash And Arugula Salad With Apple Walnut Dressing Recipe

Serving: 4 | Prep: | Cook: 30mins | Ready in:

Ingredients

- For roasted Butternut Squash:
- 1 small butternut squash
- 1/3 c. brown sugar
- 1 tsp. cinnamon
- 1 Tbs. cumin
- kosher salt and freshly ground black pepper, to taste
- 3 Tbs. melted unsalted butter

- ~~~~~~ ~~~~~~~~~~~~~~~~~~~~
- apple walnut Dressing: (can be made the day before)
- 1 Tbs. Dijon mustard
- 1 shallot, roughly chopped
- 1/2 honey Crisp apple, cored, peeled and cut in a rough dice
- 1/8 cup red wine vinegar
- 3/4 cup olive oil
- 1/4 cup chopped walnuts
- 1 Tbs. fresh thyme
- 1-2 tablespoons sugar, to taste
- Kosher salt and black pepper to taste
- ~~~~~~ ~~~~~~~~~~~~~~~~~~~~
- For salad:
- 1 carrot, julienned (I used these beautiful purple and yellow carrots from the farmer's market)
- 1 red onion, thinkly sliced and rinsed
- 1 lb. baby arugula
- 1/3 cup walnuts
- Garnish:
- Additonal toasted walnuts & pumpkin seeds, other 1/2 of apple-sliced

Direction

- For Roasted Butternut Squash:
- Preheat oven to 400°F. Cut the top off of the squash. Cut the squash into three-inch strips cutting from the top to the bottom. Spoon out the insides. Put squash in bowl and coat with butter, salt, pepper, brown sugar, cumin and cinnamon. Place on a parchment lined cookie sheet and roast in oven for 35 minutes or until tender and caramelized
- Apple Walnut Dressing:
- Use a blender to mix the Dijon mustard and vinegar for one minute. Add diced shallot, apple, sugar and thyme into the blender and blend until smooth. Slowly add the olive oil to the mixture and emulsify. Add walnuts last and only blend for a few seconds. Salt and pepper to taste.
- For salad:

- In a mixing bowl, add the carrot, red onion, and arugula. Dress the salad to taste with the apple walnut vinaigrette. Put mound of salad on each plate and top with warm butternut squash wedge. Garnish with sliced apple, the toasted pumpkin seeds and walnuts. Drizzle additional dressing around plate and serve.

---

322. Roasted Pecan Apple Salad Recipe

Serving: 4 | Prep: | Cook: 60mins | Ready in:

Ingredients

- Salad:
- 1 head red leaf lettuce
- 1 head bib leaf lettuce
- 1 C watercress
- 2 red delecious apples
- 3/4 C blue cheese
- 3/4 C roasted pecans
- roast Pecans:
- 3/4 C chopped pecans
- 1/4 C corn syrup
- 1/4 C butter
- 2T water
- 1/4 Tsp salt
- Dressing:
- 1/4 C walnut oil
- 1/4C cyder vineger
- 2T shallot (finely chopped)
- 2 T lemon juice
- 1/4 tsp salt

Direction

- Preheat oven to250
- Bring corn syrup, butter, water, and salt to boil
- Add pecans and stir a few minutes
- Spread on well-greased cookie sheet
- Bake for an hour and stir every ten minutes.
- Slice apples thin and length wise.

- Hint: when sliced place them in a bowl with cold water and cider vinegar, this will prevent them from browning.
- On individual plates place a nice big leaf of the bib lettuce. Then place the salad mixed with dressing on top. Place the thinly slice apple in a radial circle and sprinkle your roasted pecans and blue cheese.

---

323. Romaine Hazelnut Apple And Cheddar Salad Recipe

Serving: 4 | Prep: | Cook: 10mins | Ready in:

Ingredients

- 1/2 cup whole hazelnuts
- 2-1/2 tablespoons sherry wine vinegar
- 3/4 cup sunflower oil
- 1/2 teaspoon salt
- 1 teaspoon freshly ground black pepper
- 1/2 cup whole hazelnuts
- 1/2 tablespoon fresh lemon juice
- 2 granny smith apples unpeeled
- 1-1/2 pounds romaine lettuce cored cut into 1/2" wide pieces then washed and dried
- 1/2 pound sharp cheddar cheese cut into sticks

Direction

- Preheat oven to 325 then toast hazelnuts on baking sheet for 25 minutes.
- Remove from oven and immediately cover with a damp towel.
- Invert another baking sheet over the first one to hold in the steam.
- After 5 minutes remove skins from nuts then cool completely and grind in food processor.
- Transfer ground hazelnuts to a 3 quart stainless steel bowl.
- Add sherry wine vinegar and whisk to combine.
- Add safflower oil and whisk until blended then season with salt and pepper.

- Use a handheld immersion blender or a food processor to blend dressing until smooth.
- Cover with plastic wrap and set aside at room temperature until needed.
- Toast and skin remaining hazelnuts as previously described for the dressing.
- Cool to room temperature then cut in half and set aside until needed.
- In a stainless steel bowl add lemon juice to 2 cups of cold water.
- Core and quarter apples then slice and place in lemon juice mixture to prevent discoloration.
- Divide and arrange romaine pieces on four plates.
- Drain apples in a colander then rinse under cold running water and shake dry.
- Arrange apple slices around lettuce with the skin side touching or near the edge of the plate.
- Whisk the dressing then dress romaine and applies on each plate with 2 tablespoons dressing.
- Sprinkle cheddar cheese and hazelnuts on the center of each salad.
- Drizzle 2 tablespoons more of the dressing over the cheese and hazelnuts and serve immediately.

---

324. Ronnys Upgraded Waldorf Salad Recipe

Serving: 6 | Prep: | Cook: | Ready in:

Ingredients

- 3 apples
- 3 stalks of celery
- 1 can of pineapple pieces
- juice of one lemon
- 2 tablespoons of mayo'
- 1 handful of crushed walnuts
- 1 handful of raisins

Direction

- Cut the apples into small cubes
- Coarsely chop the celery
- Pour in the whole can of pineapple pieces including the syrup
- Add the lemon-juice, mayo', walnuts & raisins.
- Mix everything together well.
- Let stand in fridge for at least an hour before serving.
- Remove from fridge and give it one more toss.
- Don't be angry with yourself for not making some more. There's always next time to look forward to.

---

325. Ruby Tuesdays Apple Salad Recipe

Serving: 4 | Prep: | Cook: | Ready in:

Ingredients

- Dressing
- 1/4 cup mayonnaise
- 1/4 cup sour cream
- 2 TBS Splenda or sugar
- 1 TBS fresh lemon juice
- Salad
- 1 diced red apple
- 1 diced Granny Smith apple
- 1/3 cup chopped celery
- 1/2 cup chopped walnuts or pecans
- 1/3 cup dried cherries or cranberries
- 1 TBS fresh lemon juice
- lettuce leaves for serving

Direction

- Combine sour cream, mayonnaise, sugar and 1 TBS. lemon juice. Refrigerate until salad is prepared.
- Soak cherries or cranberries in 1/2 cup boiling water until softened, about 10 minutes. Drain well.
- Add chopped apples to a large bowl. Add 1 TBS. lemon juice and toss apples to coat. Add

celery, cherries or cranberries and nuts to the apples and mix. Add dressing, folding gently to coat all the salad ingredients.

- Chill salad for a few hours before serving.
- Serve on lettuce leaves.

326. SNICKERS AND APPLE SALAD Recipe

Serving: 8 | Prep: | Cook: |Ready in:

Ingredients

- 6 red or golden delicious apples
- 10 mini snicker bars
- 1-8 oz.container Cool Whip
- 1 C. lemon juice

Direction

- Peel, core and chop the apples into small pieces.
- Put lemon juice in bowl and then put apple pieces in the lemon juice and stir for a few seconds.
- Take out apple pieces and drain on a paper towels.
- Chop Snicker bars into small pieces.
- Mix apples and chopped Snicker bars together.
- Put into the fridge until ready to serve then mix in the Cool Whip right before serving.

327. Seared Sea Scallops With Pomegranate Dressed Salad Recipe

Serving: 8 | Prep: | Cook: 36mins |Ready in:

Ingredients

- * 2 tablespoons pomegranate molasses
- * 1/4 cup extra-virgin olive oil
- * 1/2 teaspoon ground ginger
- * 1/2 teaspoon ground fennel seed
- * Coarse salt and ground white pepper
- * 1 tablespoon vegetable oil
- * 16 medium-size scallops
- * 1 bulb fennel, tough outer leaves discarded, halved lengthwise, cored, and thinly sliced crosswise
- * 1 bunch arugula, tough stems discarded, well washed (2 cups)
- * 1 cup flat-leaf parsley leaves
- * 2 tablespoons minced chives
- * 1 ripe avocado, diced
- * 1/4 cup fresh pomegranate seeds, for garnish (optional)

Direction

- * 2 tablespoons pomegranate molasses
- * 1/4 cup extra-virgin olive oil
- * 1/2 teaspoon ground ginger
- * 1/2 teaspoon ground fennel seed
- * Coarse salt and ground white pepper
- * 1 tablespoon vegetable oil
- * 16 medium-size scallops
- * 1 bulb fennel, tough outer leaves discarded, halved lengthwise, cored, and thinly sliced crosswise
- * 1 bunch arugula, tough stems discarded, well washed (2 cups)
- * 1 cup flat-leaf parsley leaves
- * 2 tablespoons minced chives
- * 1 ripe avocado, diced
- * 1/4 cup fresh pomegranate seeds, for garnish (optional)
- Directions
- 1. In a large bowl, whisk together pomegranate molasses, olive oil, ground ginger, and ground fennel; season with salt and pepper.
- 2. In a large non-stick skillet, heat vegetable oil over medium-high heat. Season scallops with salt and pepper. When the oil is very hot, add as many scallops as will fit in a single layer, with at least 1/2 inch of space between them, and cook without turning until golden brown, 2 to 3 minutes. Turn scallops over and cook 1

133

1/2 to 2 minutes or until centers are slightly translucent. Repeat with remaining scallops.

- 3. Whisk dressing to combine. Add fennel, arugula, parsley leaves, and chives. Toss well. Add avocado and toss again. Taste and adjust seasonings if necessary.
- 4. To serve, put the salad in the center of a platter and arrange scallops on top. If desired, garnish with pomegranate seed

328. Seductive Fruit Salad Recipe

Serving: 0 | Prep: | Cook: 2hours | Ready in:

Ingredients

- Salad:
- 4 cups wild arugula
- 3 cups baby spinach
- 2 medium blood oranges, peeled and sectioned (about 1 cup)
- 10-12 fresh strawberries, hulled and sliced thin (about 1 cup)
- 1 medium mango, diced (about 1 cup)
- 1/2 cup fresh raspberries
- 1 jalapeno chopped fine
- 1/4 red onion sliced extreemly thin
- 1 tablespoon thinly sliced fresh mint leaves
- 1 tablespoon thinly sliced fresh basil leaves
- 2 tablespoons toasted nuts (such as pistachios, pecans, or walnuts)
- Vinaigrette:
- 1 tablespoon extra-virgin olive oil
- 1 tablespoon white balsamic vinegar
- 1 tablespoon fresh Meyer lemon juice (or regular lemon)
- 2 tablespoons freshly squeezed blood orange juice
- 1/4 teaspoon grated lemon zest
- salt and pepper, to taste

Direction

- To toast the nuts, place them in a small, dry skillet over medium heat. Shake the pan handle back and forth for 1-2 minutes, or until the nuts are golden brown and aromatic. Set aside.
- In a large bowl, gently toss all salad ingredients (excluding nuts).
- In a small bowl, whisk all vinaigrette ingredients until well combined. Pour over salad and toss gently until well coated. Divide the salad among four plates and sprinkle with nuts.

329. Southern Apple Beet Salad Recipe

Serving: 4 | Prep: | Cook: | Ready in:

Ingredients

- 2 cups shredded or chopped apple unpeeled
- 15 ounce can whole beets drained and chopped
- 3/4 cup sliced celery
- 1 tablespoon lemon juice
- 1 tablespoon honey
- lettuce leaves
- 3 tablespoons chopped walnuts toasted

Direction

- Combine all ingredients except lettuce leaves and walnuts tossing gently.
- Spoon out each serving onto lettuce leaves and sprinkle with walnuts to serve.

330. Spinach And Apple Salad With Warm Bacon Vinaigrette Recipe

Serving: 4 | Prep: | Cook: 10mins | Ready in:

Ingredients

- 3 Strips bacon
- 2-3 T olive oil
- 2 T red wine vinegar
- 1 t Dijon mustard
- 1 small clove garlic, minced
- 1/8 t salt
- 1 bunch (10 oz.) spinach, coarse stems trimmed (about 5 C loosely packed)
- 1 macintosh apple peeled and cut into 1/2" pieces
- 8 Shavings romano cheese, each about 1" x 2"
- 1/8 t ground black pepper

Direction

- Cook bacon in a skillet over medium-low heat, turning slices occasionally until crisp and browned. 8-10 minutes.
- Drain on paper towel-lined plate and keep warm.
- Measure the fat in pan. (There should be 2-3 T.) Add enough oil to equal 5 T of total fat in the pan.
- Whisk the vinegar, mustard, garlic, salt and pepper into the fat in pan. Keep warm.
- In a large bowl, combine the spinach and apple.
- Spoon the warm bacon mixture over the spinach and apple. Toss to coat.
- Divide among 4 plates.
- Crumble the bacon over spinach and top with the cheese.

---

331.   Spinach Raisin Pine Nut And Apple Salad Recipe

Serving: 8 | Prep: | Cook: 5mins | Ready in:

Ingredients

- 2 large bunches spinach
- 2 tablespoons olive oil
- 1/4 cup raisins

- 1/4 cup pine nuts
- 1/4 cup apples peeled and cubed
- 3-1/2 tablespoons shallots chopped
- 1/4 teaspoon salt

Direction

- Wash and dry spinach.
- Heat oil in sauté pan over medium heat.
- Cook raisins, pine nuts, apple and shallots in oil about 5 minutes stirring occasionally.
- Stir salt into raisin mixture then gradually add spinach and toss just until spinach is wilted.
- Serve immediately.

---

332.   Spinach Salad With Apple Recipe

Serving: 4 | Prep: | Cook: 30mins | Ready in:

Ingredients

- 2 tablespoons cider vinegar
- 2 tablespoons canola oil
- 1/4 teaspoon salt
- 1/4 teaspoon sugar
- 1 cup diced unpeeled apple
- 1/4 cup chopped sweet onion
- 1/4 cup craisins
- 2 cups torn fresh spinach
- 2 cups torn romaine

Direction

- Combine vinegar, oil, salt and sugar; mix well in a small bowl.
- Add apple, onion and raisins; toss lightly to coat. Cover and let stand for 10 minutes.
- Just before serving, combine spinach and romaine in a large salad bowl; add apple mix and toss. Yield: 4-6 servings.

333.   Spinach And Apple Salad Recipe

Serving: 4 | Prep: | Cook: |Ready in:

Ingredients

- 1 bag baby spinach
- 1 small head green-leaf lettuce
- 2 carrots, chopped
- 1-2 apples, cored and thinly sliced
- big handful of blanched sliced almonds
- 1/4 cup minced onion
- 3 Tbsp. cider vinegar
- 3 Tbsp. red wine vinegar
- 3 Tbsp. sugar
- 1/4 tsp. paprika
- 1-2 drops of sesame oil (don't overdo it!)
- salt and pepper to taste
- 1/4 cup olive oil

Direction

- Immediately toss apple slices with a little citrus juice (I like OJ) or vinegar to prevent browning.
- Spread almond slices on a baking sheet and toast them under the broiler or in your toaster oven. They should be well-browned (maybe even with a few burnt ones) to bring out a smoky flavor. Takes around 1-5 minutes depending on your oven -- keep an eye on them.
- Make the dressing: Whisk together sugar, vinegar, sesame oil, salt, pepper, paprika, and onion, then drizzle in olive oil while whisking to combine.
- Add salad greens, carrots, and apples to a serving bowl. Drizzle with dressing and toss.
- Top salad with toasty almond slices and serve.

334.   Stone Fruit And Berry Salad Recipe

Serving: 6 | Prep: | Cook: 30mins |Ready in:

Ingredients

- 1lb fresh plums, halved, pitted and cut into about 1/2 inch pieces
- 1lb fresh peaches, halved, pitted, and cut into about 1/2 inch pieces(leave the skin or remove it, your choice :)
- 1pt fresh blueberries
- 1pt fresh blackberries or raspberries
- juice from 1 lemon
- juice from 1 lime
- 1/4 cup honey
- 1t vanilla
- a few sprigs of fresh mint(leave whole)
- 4-6oz goat cheese with honey, crumbled

Direction

- In large bowl, combine the juices with vanilla and honey and stir to combine and mix well.
- Add all the fruits
- Rub/crush all the mint leaves on the sprigs and toss them in the bowl, too.
- Carefully fold fruit with the dressing to combine.
- Add the goat cheese crumbles and carefully fold, again.
- Refrigerate at least 2 hours or overnight.
- Remove the mint sprigs prior to serving.

335.   Strawberry Cheesecake Salad Recipe

Serving: 8 | Prep: | Cook: 10mins |Ready in:

Ingredients

- 12 ounce container Cool Whip, thawed
- 3 Strawberry Cheesecake yogurt
- 1 small package Cheesecake pudding dry mix

- 1 and 1/2 quarts fresh strawberries, cleaned, stems removed and cut into chunks
- 2 cups miniature marshmallows

Direction

- Mix together Cool Whip, yogurt and dry pudding mix until well blended.
- Stir in strawberries and marshmallows.
- Chill until ready to serve.
- Now think of ALL the different pudding flavors and fruits you could try: Banana Cream pudding mix with bananas, banana cream pie yogurt, and some crushed vanilla wafers.
- Vanilla pudding mix with apple chunks, apple pie yogurt and 1/2 cup caramel syrup.
- Lemon pudding mix with 2 cups blueberries, lemon yogurt and marshmallows.
- Come up with a new creation and let me know!

336.   Strawberry Mango Salad Recipe

Serving: 0 | Prep: | Cook: 20mins | Ready in:

Ingredients

- 1 head of romaine lettuce
- 1 cup strawberries, sliced
- 1 cup mango, diced
- 1 cup jicama, diced
- 1 avocado, diced
- 1 cup pumpkin seeds
- BLUEBERRY vinaigrette
- 1 cup blueberries
- 1T brown rice syrup or other sweetener
- 2T red wine vinegar
- 2 T of olive oil

Direction

- Tear romaine and place on plate

- Mix together fruit and jicama. Place a serving on a bed of lettuce.
- Top with Blueberry Vinaigrette and pumpkin seeds.
- VINAIGRETTE
- Combine all ingredients in a blender
- Pour over top of salad

337.   Strawberry Salad Recipe

Serving: 8 | Prep: | Cook: 10mins | Ready in:

Ingredients

- 1 small carton sour cream
- 1 - 8-12 oz. Cool Whip
- 1 - 3 oz. pkg. strawberry jello
- fresh strawberries

Direction

- Mix Cool Whip and sour cream together in bowl.
- Add dry jello from box.
- Fold in Strawberries.
- Refrigerate until ready to serve.
- Options: peaches with peach jello.

338.   Strawberry Tossed Salad Recipe

Serving: 8 | Prep: | Cook: 30mins | Ready in:

Ingredients

- Strawberry Tossed Salad
- This is a AWESOME recipe: You can serve this with Poultry,ham,and pork all throughout the year. A MUST TO TRY.
- 1/2 cup vegetable oil
- 1/3 cup sugar
- 1/4 cup cider or red wine vinegar

- 1 garlic clove,minced
- 1/4 Tsp. salt
- 1/4 tsp. paprika
- Pinch white pepper
- 8 cups torn romaine
- 4 cups torn Bibb or boston lettuce
- 2 1/2 cups sliced fresh strawberries
- 1 cup (4 ounces) shredded,
- Monterrey Jack cheese
- 1/2 cup chopped walnuts, toasted

Direction

- Combine the first seven ingredients in a jar with tight-fitting lid: Shake well. Just before serving, toss salad greens, strawberries, cheese and walnuts in a large salad bowl. Drizzle with dressing and toss.
- Yield; 6-8 servings.

---

339.   Summer Berry Chicken Salad Recipe

Serving: 0 | Prep: | Cook: 45mins | Ready in:

Ingredients

- Caramelized Walnuts:
- 1/4 c. sugar
- 1 c. walnut pieces
- (you might want to make a 2nd batch to munch on!)
- Salad:
- 3 chicken breasts, skinless & boneless
- 1 lg. apple
- 1 orange
- 6 oz. fresh raspberries
- 6 oz. fresh blackberries
- 6-8 fresh strawberries, sliced
- 3/4 bottle creamy poppyseed dressing
- 1 head romain lettuce, chopped
- Crumbled feta cheese

Direction

- Sprinkle the sugar evenly into a large skillet over medium heat. Top with walnut pieces . When sugar begins to melt, stir well to completely coat the walnuts . Turn heat to low, spread nuts evenly in skillet, and cook another 2 minutes.
- Remove to a lightly-buttered dinner plate and let cool completely.
- Grill chicken breasts & set aside . When completely cooled, slice chicken thinly.
- Core and cut apple into small pieces. (If desired, peel apple first.) Place in large bowl. Slice orange in half and squeeze all of the juice over the apple pieces. Toss to coat.
- Add the chicken and berries to the bowl and gently toss to combine (don't crush the berries). Add poppy seed dressing and toss to coat all pieces. Cover & refrigerate for 30 minutes or until ready to serve.
- To serve, spoon chicken mixture on top of chopped lettuce and toss to dress the lettuce. Sprinkle with caramelized walnuts and feta cheese.

---

340.   Summer Salad Recipe

Serving: 0 | Prep: | Cook: 30mins | Ready in:

Ingredients

- 1 nine oz package of cheese tortellini, cooked and cooled
- 1 c fresh blueberries
- 1 c fresh strawberries, sliced
- 1 c green grapes
- 1/4 c sliced almonds
- 1 can mandarin oranges, drained
- 3/4 c poppy seed dressing

Direction

- Mix pasta and salad ingredients in a large bowl.
- Pour on dressing and toss gently.
- Chill until ready to serve.

341. Sunshine Sparkle Salad Recipe

Serving: 0 | Prep: | Cook: 15mins |Ready in:

Ingredients

- 3 banana, peeled and sliced
- 2 small cans of mandarin oranges, drained juice reserved
- 1 medium can diced pineapples, drained juice reserved
- 1 jar maraschino cherries, chopped, drained juice reserved
- 12 to 15 strawberries, sliced
- 2 boxes of lemon pudding
- 1 envelope of Dream Whip
- 1/2 cup chopped pecans
- 1 cup miniature marshmallows

Direction

- In a bowl combine reserved juice,
- In a separate med sized bowl combine the pudding and dream whip, add 1 cup of reserved juice and whisk until smooth (you may have to add more since you want it more like sauce than a pudding)
- Mix the fruit together in a large bowl and slowly fold in the pudding mixture. Add pecans and fold again. Chill for at least an hour before serving.
- My daughter absolutely love it and so did my hubby. Hope you enjoy it as well.

342. Sweet Potato Salad Recipe

Serving: 0 | Prep: | Cook: 15mins |Ready in:

Ingredients

- cooked sweet potatoes, cubed
- pineapple chunks , either fresh or canned
- celery, sliced
- walnuts, chopped coarsely
- Dressing: With mayo add curry powder to taste. Stir in a little Lime juice or lemon juice.

Direction

- Gently toss together. Nice served in crisp cups of lettuce.

343. Sweet Waldorf Salad Recipe

Serving: 8 | Prep: | Cook: |Ready in:

Ingredients

- 2 granny smith apples, cored and diced
- 1 Red Delicious apple, cored and diced
- 1 Asian pear, cored and cubed
- 1 stalk celery, diced
- 1/2 cup sliced almonds
- 1 cup golden raisins
- 1 cup seedless green grapes, halved
- 1 1/2 cups sweetened dried cranberries
- -------------------------
- 1 1/4 cups plain yogurt
- 1/4 cup sugar
- 1/3 cup brown sugar
- 3/4 cup mayonnaise
- 3 Tbsp. lemon juice
- 1/2 tsp. cinnamon

Direction

- In a large bowl, combine the Granny Smith apples, Red Delicious apple, Asian pear, celery, almonds, golden raisins, grapes and cranberries. In a separate bowl, stir together the yogurt, both sugars, mayo, lemon juice and cinnamon. Pour the dressing over the fruit mixture and stir gently until evenly coated. Chill until ready to serve.

344. Syrian Fattoush Recipe

Serving: 0 | Prep: | Cook: 30mins | Ready in:

Ingredients

- A medium sized head of Roumaine lettuce
- 1 large cucumber
- 2 large yellow tomatoes
- 1 grand bunch of scallions
- 2 medium sized fire roasted bell peppers
- 1 cup of pomegranate seeds
- 1 cup flat leafed parsley (leaves only)
- 2 loaves of pita bread
- 1 cup of aged feta (I use Bulgarian)
- ¾ - 1 cup of an olive oil – red wine vinegar dressing, spiced Middle Eastern style heavy on the garlic and with fresh mint.

Direction

- Put the pomegranate seeds into the dressing and let it chill overnight.
- Chop the lettuce into a medium shred. Peel and de-seed the cucumber and chop that into a med dice. Cut the tomatoes into a slightly larger dice and chop the scallions small. Cut the red peppers into medium sized thick striplettes.
- Lightly oil and season the pita and grill it over an open flame ideally, or else in a very hot pan. A little char is acceptable. Cut it into a sixe similar to the tomato.
- Mix all the above together, and the parsley, at the very minute before serving, the bread should actually still be hot, and toss it in the dressing. Divide this evenly into some chilled bowls and sprinkle a good layer of the feta over the top.
- You can garnish with olives if you please as well.

345. Taffy Apple Salad Recipe

Serving: 8 | Prep: | Cook: | Ready in:

Ingredients

- 4 granny smith apples cubed
- 1 large can crushed pineapple in heavy syrup drained (save juice)
- 2 cups miniature marshmallows
- 1-1/2 cups cocktail peanuts
- 8 ounce container creamy Cool Whip
- 1/2 tablespoon vinegar
- 1/2 cup granulated sugar
- 1 egg
- 1 tablespoon flour

Direction

- Mix together juice, vinegar, sugar, egg and 1 tablespoon flour.
- Cook until mixture comes to a boil and is syrupy.
- Strain to remove any lumps then cool.
- Mix all ingredients and refrigerate 2 hours before serving.

346. Tropical Salad Recipe

Serving: 0 | Prep: | Cook: 15mins | Ready in:

Ingredients

- Variable to your choice but basically -
- lettuce - not too much
- Finely chopped cabbage
- Finely sliced onion
- Cherry or sliced tomatoes
- Finely sliced red pepper
- Finely sliced green pepper
- orange segments
- Sliced fresh peach
- pineapple chunks (fresh or tinned)
- Sliced apple
- kiwi fruit, peeled and sliced

- Halved grapes
- salt and pepper
- thousand island dressing

Direction

- Make a mixed salad with all the ingredients - apart from the Thousand Island Dressing
- Arrange the salad so some of the fruit is garnishing the top
- Pour a little Thousand Island Dressing over the top of the salad and serve extra in a side bowl.
- I know it sounds crazy to add this dressing to fruit - but it works.

347. Tuna Apple Salad Recipe

Serving: 4 | Prep: | Cook: | Ready in:

Ingredients

- 2 cans tuna, drain & flake (I use 1 can in oil & 1 can in water)
- 1 medium apple, diced
- 2 hard boiled eggs, chopped
- 2 Tbsp. onion, finley chopped
- 1/2-3/4 cup Mayo
- mustard, a dab
- 1/4-1/2 cup sweet relish
- salt
- pepper

Direction

- Combine and mix all ingredients in small bowl. You may want more mayo, you may want less. Season to taste. I think the more relish, the better. I like to put mine in the fridge for a while to chill a bit. Enjoy!

348. Turkey Waldorf Salad Recipe

Serving: 4 | Prep: | Cook: | Ready in:

Ingredients

- 2/3 cup mayonnaise
- 2 Tbsp lemon juice
- 1/2 tsp salt
- 1/4 tsp pepper
- 2 cups diced cooked turkey (or substitute chicken)
- 1 red apple, cored and diced
- 1 green or yellow apple, cored and diced
- 2/3 cup sliced celery
- 1/2 cup chopped walnuts
- lettuce leaves, for serving

Direction

- Mix together mayonnaise, lemon juice, salt and pepper.
- Add turkey, apples and celery to the dressing and toss until well coated.
- Cover and chill until ready to serve.
- To serve, line serving dish with crisp washed lettuce leaves. Cover with salad and top with the walnuts.

349. Uptown Chicken Waldorf Salad Recipe

Serving: 4 | Prep: | Cook: | Ready in:

Ingredients

- 2 Cups of diced cooked chicken
- 1/4 cup crumbled blue cheese
- 1/4 cup sugared pecans
- 2 granny smith apples cored and diced
- 1/4 Cup red grapes halved
- Balsamic Vinagrette (Ken's steak House)
- mixed greens

Direction

- Place greens on plate top with chicken, cheese, pecans, apples and grapes. Top with dressing according to your taste.

---

350. Waldorf Chicken Salad Recipe

Serving: 56 | Prep: | Cook: 30mins | Ready in:

Ingredients

- 1/4 cup honey
- 2 Tbps. mustard
- 1 Tbsp. poppy seeds
- 1/3 cup lemon juice
- 1/2 tsp. lemon peel, grated
- 1/4 cup vegetable oil
- 12 dried apricots, sliced
- 2 cups roasted chicken meat, cubed
- 2 apples\raw, cored and diced
- 1 cup celery\raw, diced
- 1/3 cup sliced almonds, toasted
- 1/4 cup green onions, minced

Direction

- Place first 6 ingredients in a bowl and mix well.
- Stir in apricots and let stand 30 minutes.
- Add chicken and toss lightly.
- Chill until ready to serve.
- To serve, add remaining ingredients to chicken mixture and toss well.

---

351. Waldorf Dessert Salad Recipe

Serving: 4 | Prep: | Cook: 30mins | Ready in:

Ingredients

- 1 medium red apple, unpeeled
- 1 medium green or golden apple, unpeeled
- 2 tsp lemon juice
- 1/4 cup pitted dates, chopped
- 1/2 cup seedless red grapes
- 1/2 cup seedless green grapes
- 1 can pineapple chunks, drained (approx 13 1/2 ounces)
- 1 cup miniature marshmallows
- 1/4 cup chopped pecans or walnuts
- 1/3 cup mayonnaise
- 1/3 cup sour cream

Direction

- Slice unpeeled apples in thin slices into serving bowl.
- Sprinkle lemon juice over the apple slices and toss to coat well. This will help keep the apples from turning brown.
- Add dates, grapes, pineapple, marshmallows and nuts.
- Stir mayonnaise and sour cream together in a small bowl.
- Pour over fruit and mix to coat fruit.
- Chill at least half an hour.

---

352. Waldorf Salad Recipe

Serving: 12 | Prep: | Cook: 45mins | Ready in:

Ingredients

- 6 each apple, cored, peeled and cut into 3/4 inch chunks
- 1 1/8 cups mayonnaise
- 3 teaspoons lemon rind, grated
- 1 1/2 tablespoons lemon juice
- 1 1/2 cups celery, diced small
- 3/4 cup pecan, roasted & chopped fine
- 1 1/2 cups seedless raisins
- 1 1/2 cups marshmallows, miniatures (Optional)

Direction

- Bring one cup of water to a boil in a medium saucepan. Remove from heat and stir in raisins or dried cranberries. Let stand for 10 minutes and drain.
- Roast or toast pecans in a skillet. Set aside to cool.
- Stir together all ingredients in a large salad bowl, cover and chill before serving.

353.   Waldorf Salad Recipe Recipe

Serving: 4 | Prep: | Cook: | Ready in:

Ingredients

- 1 cup chopped, slightly toasted pecans
- 1 cup celery, thinly sliced
- 1 cup red seedless grapes, sliced (or a 1/4 cup of raisins)
- 2 sweet apple, cored and chopped
- 6 Tbsp mayonnaise
- 2 Tbsp fresh lemon juice
- Salt
- pepper
- lettuce

Direction

- In a medium sized bowl, whisk together the mayonnaise (or yogurt) and the lemon juice.
- Add 1/2 teaspoon of salt, 1/4 teaspoon of fresh ground pepper.
- Mix in the apple, celery, grapes, and walnuts.
- Serve on a bed of fresh lettuce.

354.   Waldorf Salad With Turkey Recipe

Serving: 4 | Prep: | Cook: | Ready in:

Ingredients

- 2 cups leftover turkey meat, chopped or thickly sliced deli turkey, in slivers
- 2 stalks celery, sliced
- 1/3 cup flat leaf parsely, chopped
- 1 crisp apple,whatever is your favorite
- 1 cup golden raisins or craisins
- 1/4 cup mayonnaise
- 1/2 cup plain yogurt
- 2 Tbsp. brown sugar
- salt to taste
- 1 teas. poppy seeds
- lettuce cups to serve in for garnish

Direction

- In a large salad bowl combine chopped or slivered turkey, celery, parsley, apple, raisins or craisins. In a separate bowl combine mayonnaise, yogurt, brown sugar, salt and poppy seeds. Whisk well to combine.
- Add dressing to turkey ingredients and mix well. Chill for 1 hour. Serve in lettuce leaves on a pretty plate!

355.   Waldorf Summer Chicken Salad Recipe

Serving: 4 | Prep: | Cook: 10mins | Ready in:

Ingredients

- 1 pound red apples, diced or sliced
- 3 Tbs. fresh lemon juice
- 2/3 cup light mayonnaise
- 1 stalk of celery
- 4 shallots, sliced
- 1 garlic clove, crushed
- 3/4 cup chopped walnuts
- 1 pound cooked chicken, cubed
- 1 head romaine lettuce
- pepper

Direction

- Place the apples in a bowl with the lemon juice and 1 tbs. of mayonnaise. Set aside for 40 minutes.
- Slice the celery very thinly.
- Add celery with the shallots, garlic, and walnuts to the apple. Mix, then add the remaining mayonnaise, and blend thoroughly.
- Add the chicken, mix, and line a glass salad bowl or serving dish with the lettuce.
- Pile the chicken salad into the center, sprinkle with pepper, and garnish with apple slices and walnuts.

356. Water Melon & Feta Salad Recipe

Serving: 0 | Prep: | Cook: 15mins | Ready in:

Ingredients

- 1/2 water melon try some sweet n seedless
- 200 gms of feta
- salt n pepper to taste
- 80ml of olive oil
- some basil leaves for garnish

Direction

- Wash n cut the melon into 1/2 then with a scooper or a spoon scoop out some lovely round balls of watermelon or u cut into chunks it totally depends on you.
- In a mixing bowl add olive oil salt n pepper n just mix it a kind of dressing pour it on the water melon n let chill for couple of hour
- Before serving just add crumble feta n garnish with basil leaves try not to use knife to the cut leaves just with pluck it with hands
- Ready to serve. Can be served in the watermelon shell.
- Enjoy:-P
- Ps: if u like my recipes please rate it!!!! Thank you

357. Watercress Citrus Salad With Grilled Figs Recipe

Serving: 4 | Prep: | Cook: 15mins | Ready in:

Ingredients

- 1 can (15 ounces) Kadota figs in light syrup, drained and halved
- 1/4 cup vinaigrette dressing, divided
- 3 bunches watercress, trimmed
- 1 can (6 ounces) mandarin oranges, drained
- 2 tablespoons chopped chives
- 1/2 teaspoon fresh thyme
- 1/2 teaspoon fresh tarragon
- 1/4 cup toasted pine nuts or slivered almonds
- 1/4 cup crumbled feta cheese, optional
- Freshly grated pepper, to taste

Direction

- Preparation Time: Approximately 15 minutes
- Preparation:
- In a medium bowl gently toss figs with 2 tablespoons vinaigrette dressing; marinate for 10 minutes. Grill under broiler on high heat just until lightly browned; set aside. Meanwhile, put 2 tablespoons vinaigrette dressing, watercress, Mandarin oranges, chives, thyme and tarragon in a salad bowl. Toss gently. Arrange on salad plates, top with figs, pine nuts, feta cheese and pepper.
- Servings: 4
- Nutritional Information Per Serving: Calories 180; Total fat 8g; Saturated fat 0g; Cholesterol 0mg; Sodium 150mg; Carbohydrate 27g; Fiber 1g; Protein 4g; Vitamin A 90%DV*; Vitamin C 90%DV; Calcium 15%DV; Iron 6%DV

358. Watermelon Feta Salad Recipe

Serving: 0 | Prep: | Cook: 30mins | Ready in:

Ingredients

- 2 1/2 cups chilled watermelon, cut into small cubes
- 1/4 cup fresh mint leaves, finely chopped
- 4 tsp. fresh chives, finely chopped
- 1/4 cup finely crumbled feta cheese (or to taste if you like more feta)
- 2 tbsp. balsamic vinegar reduction
- cracked pepper to taste
- Balsamic Reduction:
- 1 cup balsamic vinegar

Direction

- Pour the balsamic vinegar in a small saucepan and cook over medium heat until reduced by half. Cool before use. Set aside.
- Place watermelon cubes in a bowl.
- Sprinkle cubes with mint, chives and feta.
- Drizzle with balsamic reduction. (I left this on the side so guests could put on how much they wanted)
- Sprinkle with fresh cracked black pepper.
- Enjoy.

---

359.   Watermelon Salad Recipe

Serving: 4 | Prep: | Cook: 10mins | Ready in:

Ingredients

- 2 to 3 cups watermelon in bite-sized chunks, seeds removed
- 2 small ripe tomatoes, quartered
- 2 to 3 ounces fresh goat cheese, crumbled
- 2 tablespoons prepared balsamic vinaigrette dressing
- 2 to 3 tablespoons chopped fresh basil

Direction

- On a large platter or individual plates, arrange watermelon, tomatoes and goat cheese. Drizzle with vinaigrette

---

360.   Watermelon Shark

Serving: 25 | Prep: | Cook: 1hours | Ready in:

Ingredients

- 1 large watermelon
- 2 cups seedless red grapes
- 1 medium cantaloupe, peeled, seeded and cubed
- 2 cups fresh blueberries
- 2 medium oranges
- 1 jar (12 ounces) pineapple preserves
- Swedish Fish candies, optional

Direction

- Using a large sharp knife, cut off one end of the watermelon so that watermelon stands at an angle. Using a razor blade or small knife, score an opening for the mouth. With knife, cut out and remove mouth. Cut out triangles for teeth; remove rind from teeth.
- For shark fin, cut a triangle from removed rind; attach to shark with toothpicks. For eyes, attach two grapes with toothpicks.
- Remove fruit from inside watermelon; cut into cubes. In a large bowl, combine watermelon, cantaloupe, blueberries and remaining grapes. Finely grate peel from oranges and squeeze juice. In a small bowl, mix preserves, orange juice and peel; add to fruit and toss gently.
- Stand shark on a platter. Fill opening with some of the fruit mixture; add a few Swedish Fish if desired. Serve with remaining fruit.
- Nutrition Facts
- 3/4 cup (calculated without candies): 129 calories, 1g fat (0 saturated fat), 0 cholesterol, 7mg sodium, 30g carbohydrate (28g sugars, 2g fiber), 2g protein. Diabetic Exchanges: 1-1/2 fruit, 1/2 starch.

361.   Watermelon, Arugula, And Pine Nut Salad

Serving: 6 | Prep: | Cook: 10mins | Ready in:

Ingredients

- 1 tablespoon fresh lemon juice
- 1 tablespoon red-wine vinegar
- 1/2 teaspoon table salt, or to taste
- 2 tablespoons extra-virgin olive oil
- 3 cups cubed (1/2 to 3/4 inch) seeded watermelon, drained (from a 2 1/2-lb piece, rind discarded)
- 6 cups baby arugula (6 oz)
- 1/4 cup pine nuts (1 oz)
- 1/3 cup crumbled feta or ricotta salata (1 1/2 oz)
- Coarsely ground black pepper to taste
- Fleur de sel to taste (optional)

Direction

- Whisk together lemon juice, vinegar, and salt in a large bowl, then add oil in a slow stream, whisking until emulsified.
- Add watermelon, arugula, and pine nuts and toss to coat, then sprinkle with cheese, pepper, and fleur de sel (if using).

362.   Watermelon, Feta & Mint Salad Recipe

Serving: 4 | Prep: | Cook: 10mins | Ready in:

Ingredients

- 3 1/2 cups seedless watermelon cut in 1 1/2 inch chunks or scooped balls (using melonballer)
- 4 oz. or 1 1/2 cups feta cheese, cut in about 1/2 inch cubes
- 1 tbsp olive oil
- 1 tbsp orange muscat champagne vinegar (Trader Joe's)
- 3 tbsp fresh mint leaves, coarsely chopped

Direction

- Combine watermelon and feta in a bowl. In a separate bowl, combine olive oil, vinegar, and mint leaves. Mix well. Pour over watermelon & feta. Toss gently to coat. Serve or chill until desired temperature is reached.

363.   Wonderful And Yummy Waldorf Salad With A Twist Recipe

Serving: 8 | Prep: | Cook: | Ready in:

Ingredients

- Wonderful and yummy Waldorf Salad with a twist
- 3 CUPS apples (use any type you like, or a combination)
- 1 CUP walnuts or pecans, or a combination of both
- 1 cup red or green seedless grapes, halved (or fourths) or a combination of both
- 2/3 CUP chopped celery or cut in very thin half moons
- 1 CUP walnuts or pecans, or a combination of both
- 1- 8 ounce package (SOFT) cream cheese with 2 tbls. high
- quality mayonnaise.
- (you may also sub plain yogurt (if desired!)
- 1/2 lemon- juice- to retard discoleration
- 1 tbls sugar
- We like to add a few marachino sweet cherries also..(almost forgot
- them) optional

Direction

- Wash and core the apples, leaving the skins on.

- Chop into pieces that are slightly smaller than bite-sized and place in a large bowl.
- Clean celery and cut off bottoms. Chop and add them to the chopped apples.
- Add nuts and grapes to the apples and celery.
- Mix (SOFT) cream cheese with mayonnaise.
- (To desired consistency).
- Add cheese mixture to the apple mixture and fold together until the apple mixture is well coated.
- Can be eaten immediately, but is better if refrigerated for a few hours.
- Serve on a lettuce leaf or over a bed of chopped lettuce. (Bibb lettuce looks really nice!)

364. Cranberry Apple Salad Recipe

Serving: 1012 | Prep: | Cook: | Ready in:

Ingredients

- 2- cans [1lb. each] whole berry cranberrt sauce
- 2 cup boiling water
- 2 pkg [3 oz each] strawberry flavored gelatin
- 2 tbl lemon juice
- 1/2 tea salt
- 1 cup mayonnaise
- 2cup diced apple
- 1/ cupchopped walnuts

Direction

- Melt cranberry sauce over medium heat.
- Drain, reserving liquid and berries.
- Mix together cranberry liquid, boiling water and gelatin; stir until gelatin is dissolved. Add lemon juice and salt, chill until mixture mounds slightly on a spoon. Add mayo; beat till smooth. Fold in cranberries, apple, and nuts.
- Pour into 2-quart mold. Chill overnight

365. Oriental Gingered Apple Salad Recipe

Serving: 6 | Prep: | Cook: | Ready in:

Ingredients

- 3 cups diced unpeeled apples
- 1 (8 oz) can water chestnuts, drained and diced
- 3/4 cup finely diced celery
- 1/2 cup dried cranberries
- 1/2 cup lowfat vanilla yogurt
- 1/4 cup light mayonnaise
- 1/2 tsp. ground ginger
- 2 Tbs. sugar
- 1/8 tsp. salt
- 1/4 cup chopped pecans, toasted

Direction

- In a bowl, combine apples, water chestnuts, celery, and cranberries.
- Stir together yogurt, mayonnaise, ginger, sugar, and salt.
- Pour over apple mixture and toss to coat.
- Sprinkle with pecans.

Index

A

Almond 3,4,5,6,9,26,33,76,87,93,109

Apple 3,5,6,7,8,10,73,76,77,78,79,80,81,82,83,84,85,86,87,88,89,90,93,94,96,97,98,99,100,101,102,103,104,106,107,108,109,110,112,113,114,116,122,124,127,129,130,131,132,134,135,136,140,141,147

Apricot 5,6,78,85,88

Artichoke 3,10

Asparagus 3,6,7,12,89,127

Avocado 3,4,5,6,7,12,13,17,27,34,78,91,92,99,122

B

Bacon 4,5,6,7,8,48,56,79,87,88,95,122,134

Baking 41

Banana 5,6,79,86,92,93,137

Basil 7,111,125

Berry 6,7,8,94,118,136,138

Blueberry 6,91,137

Bread 4,49

Brie 5,62,70,79

Broccoli 3,6,14,91,94,95

Butter 7,106,130

C

Cabbage 6,7,96,97,117,129

Camembert 5,79

Caramel 6,58,98,138

Carrot 3,4,6,21,39,98,99

Cashew 4,6,7,51,94,121

Cauliflower 6,95

C (continued)

Celery 5,77

Champ 6,7,44,99,122

Cheddar 7,129,131

Cheese 3,4,5,6,7,8,19,26,40,44,46,47,48,58,60,63,67,68,71,74,76,80,83,87,99,101,102,110,113,122,136

Cherry 4,6,7,52,99,100,127,140

Chicken 3,4,5,6,7,8,15,16,17,28,32,34,35,41,42,45,80,89,100,101,102,103,115,120,138,141,142,143

Chilli 124

Cinnamon 4,6,31,83,103

Clementine 3,4,16,18,41

Cocktail 7,120

Cola 4,7,35,125

Couscous 6,103

Crab 4,6,50,51,104

Cranberry 4,5,6,7,8,33,52,61,63,69,72,81,104,105,116,147

Cream 4,6,7,40,50,90,92,106,137

Crumble 4,40,44,53,57,71,73,87,88,135,138

Cucumber 3,6,7,18,97,107

Cumin 3,27

Curry 23

D

Date 3,18

Dijon mustard 28,31,37,38,43,45,51,54,59,60,64,68,69,70,71,74,77,79,80,87,92,94,99,101,102,110,114,115,118,121,122,123,129,130,135

Duck 5,74

F

Fat 3,8,17,20,27,42,61,85,96,140

Fennel 3,4,5,6,7,16,26,32,43,49,55,77,85,99,110

Feta 3,4,5,7,8,18,40,81,110,122,144,146

Conclusion

Thank you again for downloading this book!

I hope you enjoyed reading about my book!

If you enjoyed this book, please take the time to share your thoughts and post a review on Amazon. It'd be greatly appreciated!

Write me an honest review about the book – I truly value your opinion and thoughts and I will incorporate them into my next book, which is already underway.

Thank you!

If you have any questions, **feel free to contact at:** *author@fetarecipes.com*

Lena Jones

fetarecipes.com

Printed in the USA
CPSIA information can be obtained
at www.ICGtesting.com
LVHW072131281223
767702LV00025B/609